Raft of Life

A Collaborative Novel.

Raft of Life

A Collaborative Novel.

Edited by John Goodwin.

Editor's Note.

This project was compiled and formatted by the editor through a series of meetings during which the contributors undertook role play and discussion to integrate the original concurrently written short stories into a cohesive novel based on a scenario created by John Goodwin.

Writing groups interested in this exercise, may wish to contact the Paphos Writers Group for more details. Please apply through the PWG website: www.paphoswritersgroup.com

iv

Raft of Life

First Printing: 2015

ISBN 978-0-9574523-5-0

Published by

Anixe Publishing Ltd
77 Ridgeway Avenue
Gravesend, Kent DA12

www.anixepublishing.co.uk

Ordering Information:
Special discounts are available on quantity purchases
by corporations, associations, educators, and others.
For details, contact the publisher at the above listed
address.

All trade bookstores and wholesalers: Please contact
Anixe Publishing Ltd

Tel: 00357 26622279; or email anixe@jgoodwin.info

Dedication

This book is dedicated to Eleni Protopapas and Brian Hodgkinson who both sadly passed away before seeing their contribution published.

x

Acknowledgements

WITH THANKS to the Paphos Writers Group for their encouragement and support.

Cover picture by Lightning Source

In this experiment in large group, collaborative writing by members of the Paphos Writers Group each of the main chapters was written concurrently and merged around a broad framework to form a single manuscript later. The project was undertaken in response to "The National Novel Writing Month (NaNoWriMo)," November 2012.

The Cast in Order of Appearance.

Caroline Cavendish	The Lawyer	by	Frances Tomkinson
Jenni Carter	The Cruise Director	by	Nikki Burrows
Diana Somers	The Dancer	by	Dee Leigh
Ken Watts	The Policeman	by	Dee Leigh
Clarissa Sparrow	The Sparrow	by	Gloria Cuthbert
Ted Turney	The Orator	by	Luke Godson
Julia Pemberton	The Divorcee	by	Catherine Wells
Francesca Morton	The Teenager	by	Andie Haynes
Isobel James	The Pensioner	by	Sue Leese
Adam Stone	The Soldier	by	John Goodwin
D.J Postlethwaite	The Entrepreneur	by	Dorothy Bowman
Antonio McBride	The Waiter	by	John Goodwin
Jack Brownlow	The Convict	by	Brian Hodgkinson
Helena Papas	The Cypriot	by	Eleni Protopapas
Rev. Goodfellow	The Vicar	by	Gloria Cuthbert

Contents

Chapter 1

Three days out on the seven-day trip from Fort Lauderdale, Florida to Bermuda the small but luxurious cruise ship "Ocean Eco Star" struck, or was struck by, an underwater object and started rapidly sinking. She was about 700 kilometres from the nearest land, just inside the Bermuda Triangle.

It was early evening and most of the 700 passengers, all adults as there were no children's facilities, were at dinner at the time and oblivious to the thick fog that had enveloped the ship.

All at Sea

The deck lurched dangerously once more. Caz slithered in bare feet and managed to stay upright. She'd been searching; knowing her time was up. She didn't need instinct to understand that the ship would go down any minute, it was obvious. The cabin she shared with her mother was on the highest level, maybe she could still get there. She had to try; couldn't leave her mother, who might have passed out from the combination of wine and tranquillisers she'd consumed at dinner. Caz peered down into the dark of the staircase, which lay now at an odd angle. She found the handrail and grasped it with both hands, feeling her way with her feet. But after only a few precarious steps, there was water lapping at her ankles.

1

'No. No. Please no. Mum! Mum where are you?' Her cry turned into a scream, which reverberated against the walls of the stricken staircase. Caz was hardly aware whose voice it was.

She felt a tugging at her arm and a deep voice urging her back.

'It's too late. Hurry, we can still make it to the last raft.'

'But my mother. My mother's down there,' she cried.

'She'll be on one of the lifeboats. The crew searched all the cabins. Come.'

Strong arms hauled her back up the stairs and prevented her from tripping on her long dress.

'You'll have to get that off. It'll drag you down. We've got to swim. All the boats have gone.'

Caz stared blankly into blue eyes. The man nodded and she obeyed like an automaton. What did it matter if she lost her dress? Her shoes were gone and so was her mother.

'Oh God, Mum.'

She found herself being dragged up the deck, which was now at a good 45 degrees. They climbed over the rail together and before she could think about what leaping from that height meant, the man grabbed her hand and shouted 'Jump!'

The fall seemed to last forever, but all she was aware of was the air rushing past her body and the comfort of a stranger's hand. The impact of the water shocked her into survival mode and she came to the surface fighting for her life. He was still there, treading water, grabbing for her.

'I can swim.' She yelled over the roar of the waves and the sinking ship. He pointed and after a moment Caz could just make out the shape of a life raft bobbing in the dark about twenty yards away. They struck out for it together, matching stroke for stroke. She had swum for her school and might have taken it up seriously at one point, before her life had been mapped out for her.

He pulled himself up and into the raft first and then reached down into the dark sea for her, helping her up. It was confusing in there. There seemed to be legs and bodies all around but at last, the two of them sank down onto the floor. A number of voices spoke all at once, some reassuring and some hysterical. There was a glimmer of light and Caz turned to the man who had saved her life, taking in a strong body and kind, sympathetic eyes.

It was only then that she realised she was sitting there in soaked, skimpy underwear. Caz could sometimes be a flirt, but she was not, what she termed "a flaunter". She pulled her arms across her body.

'It's all right,' he said. 'We're alive . . . for now. You're a good swimmer.'

***

It had been an hour since they had heard any voices from the other lifeboats. The fog rolled around them condensing in rivulets on the canvas canopy of the inflatable life raft. It seemed to muffle out all sound as well as blanking out the moon and stars. The dozen or so occupants huddled into themselves soaking wet and shivering. If they had made it into the proper lifeboats, they would at least be dry.

The passengers only knew that the ship came to a shuddering stop with a loud bang and started rapidly sinking. In the confusion that followed, a small group of stragglers failed to make it into the ships lifeboats and, having jumped into the sea, made their way onto an inflatable liferaft. Among their number were three crew members. The most senior of these was the Assistant Cruise Director. Although employed as part of the entertainment staff, her responsibility was to pay particular attention to the emergency training courses, so she now took charge.

Her role now was to set an example, ensure safety aboard the diminutive craft and keep the peace until rescuers arrived. It was only as she had settled the last of her sea-soaked charges into the life raft, that Jenni (that's Jenni without an "e" as she always insisted) could ease herself and her damp clothes into a sitting position close to the roll down canvas hatch. Having finished ensuring that each and every one had swallowed both of their sea sickness tablets, inspecting their unwilling mouths, she desperately tried to take up a lady-like pose. She shoved a packet deep into her pocket which was hard as she had been wearing her skirted dress uniform when the call to muster stations came. The life-raft rocked, as she completed regaling her charges with precise instructions as per her training.

Shining a torch towards her face, she began. 'Ladies and gentlemen if you please,' Jenni coughed, allowing a short interval, and pushed the rats tails of her wet strawberry blond hair behind her ears. Once they were all seated, settled and paying attention, she continued to speak, raising her voice, which was being muffled by the confined space and rubber walls.

'Many of you will recognise me from the stage shows and sail-away parties, but for those who missed them and my ugly mug-shot on the reception deck wall, I am Jenni Carter, the Ship's Assistant Cruise Director. As such, I am afraid, I am in charge of this most luxuriously appointed vessel.

'Now, we will be able to move around, though obviously one at a time and with care. The raft will take plenty of pummelling, but not much in the way of jumping about. I need to take your names for the records, and if we all take a few moments to introduce ourselves, then it will make our time together so much more pleasant. No life stories, just a quick introduction and tell me where you were when you were first aware that the ship was in trouble. These things can only help the company's disaster planning in the future.

'As I said, I am Jenni. I'm also a qualified first aider, so if you have any minor cuts, abrasions or any other health problems, please let me know. We have quite an extensive first aid kit. I do need to know if any of you are diabetic, take any prescription medicines, or have any allergies, which could affect you. I do hope you heeded the instructions to bring all pills and potions with you.'

'I have a latex allergy,' piped up one of the passengers, 'I'm a bit concerned about touching the boat'.

'That won't be a problem,' Jenni responded with a kind smile, 'there's no latex in the make-up of the raft; it's all synthetic rubber.

Now, we will try to dry our clothes when this fog clears, but for now, please loosen anything that is tight, rubs or chafes, as the salt water can make you quite sore'.

Jenni paused to count her charges and to make a note on a waterproof clipboard she had removed from a pocket in the craft's wall.

'I see there are fourteen of us in all. This raft is designed for up to twenty, so we do have some spare drinking water and emergency supplies, but I will be in charge of rationing and must be strict although I am sure we will not be aboard long. Distress signals have gone out from the ship, and we are equipped with a radio beacon and flares. As you can see, there are ventilation and observation ports, and even pockets, which we can fill with water if we need more ballast. The skin of the raft is double to minimise the chances of puncture, but I must ask you to throw anything sharp overboard as we really cannot take the risk.' At this point, most of the group shook their heads, but there was a shuffle from a young female whose face was only partially illuminated by the battery lantern behind her shoulder.

'Is that you Diana?' Jenni asked, 'now you don't have anything sharp in that overstuffed bag of yours do you Di?' The girl shook her head. 'She's one of our dancers you know,' the officer added rather sarcastically.

The girl had forced an embarrassed smile as she boarded the life raft. Having had no time to change then, fully aware that she had an audience even in this impromptu situation, the smile was replaced with a theatrical grin. This was all she had ever known in her world of sycophants, glittering costumes, Leichner makeup, scuffed toed ballet shoes, worn out tap shoes, evocative music, and a tirade of shallow minded admirers. Even the soaking wet and straggly, the thigh length cheap faux fur coat she wore appeared to be a metaphor for the masquerade of the life she had chosen to inhabit. She would not consider wearing the real thing as that would challenge her moral ethic against animal cruelty. Yet despite the lack lustre coat, she could not hide the tantalising flesh, the ample bosom, flat stomach and long legs. To complete her overall allure, a jaunty black cap to protect her wet hair.

The sparkling bikini she wore, under the coat that once dazzled and danced, in the beam of a super trouper, on the stage now faded. Her tattered fish nets and on one foot a heelless shoe that squelched salt water between her toes uncomfortably as she tried to hobble about. She threw down the heavy holdall bag from her shoulder and the raft swayed then corrected itself.

A bearded middle aged man with a midlands accent said 'Do you really need that bag to be so large? We don't have a lot of room as it is.'

Diana got a whiff of alcohol as he spoke, her father drifted into her thoughts, and she shivered as she responded in her delectable lilting Irish accent.

'Like all women my life is in this bag,' she said with a girlish giggle, trying not to show any malice towards this man.

In her left hand, she carried a stiletto shoe by the strap. In her coat pocket was a small, floppy eared, teddy bear. Feeling very self-conscious, particularly because of the males on board, she covered herself by folding her coat around her tightly and looked for somewhere to sit.

'At least she had the sense not to wear the other dagger heeled shoe or we would be all shark meat by now,' venomously interjected the woman with the very red hair and vivid green eyes.

'Cost me a month's wages to buy these,' she said, holding the intact one up for all to see, and look at them . . . so much for Florida Keys finest.' There was no response.

Diana kept apologising, as she scrambled about until she finally found a place to sit, squeezing between two male passengers.

'That's no problem my love,' said one of them, 'no problem at all'. He seemed a pleasant man, with a certain military bearing, and strong Yorkshire accent. He could see Diana was feeling uncomfortable with the remarks, and promptly set about to dispel any possible volatile situation that could arise. 'In my experience, the philosophy of this situation is to remain calm. It does no good creating any other unwelcome scenarios. Let's leave the turbulence to the sea, where it belongs, shall we?'

'Jasus, makes me remember that rhyme so appropriate, "God is good but never dance on a small boat"' Diana enthused squeezing herself tighter between the two men. 'Sounds like you have done this before.' they shook hands 'Diana Somers, let me just . . .' Putting the bag between her legs, caused more rocking.

'Tut, tut, that bag of yours is far too big young woman; why you need to carry so much is beyond me,' complained an elderly woman sitting opposite her.

Silence and rage hung in the balance in the chilly, emotionally charged atmosphere. Seething, Diana thought, *If this woman say's another word to me, I swear I'll . . . I'll . . .* As she leaned forward the bear fell out of the pocket, all frayed and wet. Picking him up and pressing him close to her, she kissed him on his wet nose.

Looking around the raft, she recognised Jenni, of course, and a passenger who had introduced himself once as Ted something or other. She has seen him on a few occasions. Another man she recognised, despite his hand covering the left side of his face, was sitting with the red head the woman who looked to be in her forties. Diana, even though only three days into the cruise, had a good memory for faces. Especially those that are male with groping hands and old fashioned chat up lines. She settled into her place hugging the little bear to her neck, closed her eyes and shivered.

***

People were shuffling about trying to get comfortable and not paying much attention but Jenni knew she would have to keep them focused until they were properly organised.

'Everyone . . .' She raised her voice to get their attention, 'we will need to take it in turns to be on lookout but before we set up a watch rota, let's start by introducing ourselves shall we? You Sir, the gentleman seated next to Diana there in that dark corner, what's your name?'

His voice was warm and clear as he said, 'Me? I'm Ted Turney.' He shuffled his long legs. Despite the circumstances, he still looked smart in his wet tuxedo, even without a tie. His unlined face attempted a smile as he continued, 'I wish I could say it was nice to be here with you all.'

'Thank you Ted, and you girl?' Jenni focussed on the next person round. There was no response.

'Don't you worry my dear, you're safe now,' Ted said encouragingly.

'Oh come on girl we haven't got all day. Pull yourself together,' a woman sitting opposite her groaned a reproach at the youngster.

Ted put a comforting arm around the girl's slim and shaking shoulders, while aiming a reproachful look towards the antagonist.

'As we are all destined to spend time together, why don't you tell us about yourself,' he continued kindly. 'Will you tell us your name?'

She peeked up, shyly this time. 'Francesca . . . Francesca Morton. My mother doesn't . . . didn't like anyone to shorten it but all my friends call me Franny.' She was desperate for the loo, surprising as very little fluid had passed her lips recently. But she certainly didn't fancy asking what she should do about it.

Ted let the change to past tense go for now. Time for disclosures of that magnitude later.

Having calmed the girl, he discreetly, consigned her to the older woman who sat next along. Crawling away he said, 'Would you like me to take first watch, Jenni? I'll be able to hear the other introductions just as well if I'm sitting in the hatch and in this fog . . .'

'Good man, Ted . . . so now you madam?' Jenni gestured at the woman who was tenderly cradling the teenager.

Gradually the woman became aware of the rest of her fellow survivors but she didn't recognize any of them, hardly surprising since she'd barely spoken to anyone since boarding the cruise liner. 'My name is Isobel . . . Isobel James,' she said, 'I was one of the last passengers to struggle onto this thing.' She was a rather plump lady, of about sixty years of age, with severely cropped mousy hair and hazel eyes.

'I didn't think I was going to make it! This dress, you know, and I don't swim very well.' The dress in question was made of deep crimson velvet with voluminous, richly embroidered skirts. It would obviously have hampered her progress through the water and now clung to her chunky legs.

'What on Earth do you think happened? Did we hit something? As soon as I saw that awful fog I knew something disastrous would happen!' She struggled to make herself comfortable.

Some of the passengers were arguing about what had happened. Others, like her, were stunned into silence. In any case, whatever the cause of the disaster, here they were. Literally all in the same boat!

The motley collection of assembled passengers and crew all looked to the officer for explanations, but Jenni was clearly as bewildered about the cause of the sudden sinking as they. Her office, where she had been organising the next week's rota, was amidships and had no view of the sea.

One particularly vociferous character was demanding to know if there had been a bomb on board.

'Sorry, I'm afraid I have absolutely no idea what happened.' She shrugged. Secretly she wondered if terrorism might actually be involved. Whatever her concerns, she tried to keep her tone light. 'The ship had the latest technology aboard, so we won't be here long, I'm sure. Now would you mind quietening down so that I can get the formalities out of the way? What is your name, for the record?'

He puffed out his chest with a look of sheer arrogance and replied loudly, 'Major Adam Stone.'

Jotting it down, with deliberate lack of reaction, Jenni looked round the dim interior. 'Now who haven't we heard from . . . You sir?'

'I'm D. J Postlethwaite, my family call me David. I was . . .'

The introductions were interrupted by Ted's cry of alarm.

'There's someone in the water!'

'Where?' The life raft rocked alarmingly as some of the occupants scrambled to the open flap in the canopy.

'Look.' He pointed through the murk at a tuft of white that appeared sporadically on the otherwise oily sea.

'Hey . . . over here.' Jenni shouted and waved.'

'He's not wearing a life jacket . . . I don't think he'll . . .' Ted was pushed out of the way as Caz forced her slim frame into the opening.

'He's drowning . . . here hold this . . .' She stripped off her lifejacket handing it behind, dived in and swam powerfully in the direction of the splashes. 'Can you still see him?' She started to turn on the spot, treading water.

'No . . . wait . . . yes, a few yards behind you, I think . . . The fog is so thick.' Ted had clambered out of the raft and stood clinging to the canopy.

'This way?'

'Yes can't you see him?'

'Yeah . . . I think so'

'Caz, what the hell are you doing? You idiot . . .' Jenni turned to the others, 'she'll drown too if she doesn't look out.' she clambered back inside.

'I've got him . . . throw me a line.' Caz spluttered.

'Out of the way,' Jenni pushed into the group at the opening and standing awkwardly on the yielding rubber float hurled a large quoit, with a white streamer of heaving line trailing behind it, at the struggling couple in the water. Caz hooked her arm into the quoit, and they hauled her back to the raft.

'Here, give me a hand.' Caz pushed the rescued man up to the opening. 'He seems to have passed out.'

Ted reached over the side, grabbed hold of the man's white jacket, and heaved. 'He's holding on to something. I can't get him in.'

'Hang on,' Caz swam round and prised the man's fingers from the handle of a large red duffle bag that he was hanging onto as if his life depended on it. 'Ok, now heave,'

'That's it, we've got him. Now you'd better climb up, there's a sort of step thing there just under the water.'

'Right but take this bag off me it might be useful.'

By the time Caz had clambered aboard, a woman was giving the man mouth to mouth.

He spluttered, splashing her face with snot and salty water.

'Yuck,' she said, as she withdrew. Placing a hand on his chest as she pushed back elicited a cry of agony from the man. 'Oh sorry, are you hurt?'

The man ran his hand over the front of his white bolero jacket, groaned and said, 'It's my ribs I got a bit crushed by one of the jammed lifeboats. I was trying to get one of the tote bags out. I had it when I went into the sea.'

'You still had it when we pulled you in.' Ted said, as he eased through the hatchway.

'Where?'

'It's all right, we have it here . . . what is it anyway?'

'Open it up it's full of provisions, water and things; they keep them on the lifeboats.' He heaved himself backwards to sit up resting against the inflated side of the raft alongside a greying middle aged man and looked around at the concerned faces. 'Hello everyone,' he grinned crinkling up the laughter lines on his deeply tanned face. 'Thanks for saving me. I was about to call it a day just then.'

'So what's your name, son?' a man asked.

'Oh hi, Mr Watts, it's Tony. I was your waiter when you first came on board, don't you remember?' Tony grinned again, 'You got me demoted because I spilled the soup.' He looked around for sympathy in the eyes of the other survivors but found little. 'I guess

14

I'm unemployed now anyway.' He laughed and shook his head. Dark curls, stiff with dried seawater, wobbled like coiled springs. 'Am I too late for breakfast?'

Once the new survivor had been made comfortable, Jenni picked up where she had left off.

'We were just introducing ourselves, I'm Ms Carter, the only officer on the raft, I don't think we have met before, have we?'

'Not face to face I suppose,' replied the tanned and handsome young man in the white uniform jacket as he eased himself painfully back against the rubber walls.

'Well, introduce yourself to your companions; we may be cooped up here for quite some time.'

'Hello everyone,' he said. 'My name is Antonio McBride.' He spoke softly in his diluted Scottish accent. 'As I said to Mr Watts, I was a waiter on the ship. Most people call me Tony.'

'Hi, son, I'm Ted,' Turney poked his head in from his lookout position. 'We're all in this together now you know.'

'Thanks Ted. Can you see anything out there?'

'Nothing . . . visibility is about ten metres or so now, but I think the fog is lifting slightly.'

'Now you?' Jenni tapped the knee of the woman that had been so disparaging about towards Franny. Having taken advantage of the reshuffle while tony was brought on board she was now sitting in one corner of the rectangular covered space on the raft.

'Julia Pemberton,' she replied in such a way that it was clear she did not want to be involved in any further conversation. She closed her eyes and returned

15

to her own thoughts. Her Givenchy gown was sodden and torn. Even worse, she had been obliged to abandon her Jimmy Choo's. Yet Julia retained her poise and appeared resigned to the current crisis unfolding in the lifeboat. She was relieved that she had mostly kept her head above water, allowing her makeup, which had been skilfully applied earlier that evening, to remain intact. She flicked her fingers through her damp tousled brown locks, which framed her heart shaped face.

Each night on the cruise, she had dressed to impress; after all, she was always seated at the Captain's table, thanks to Daddy's networking. She had revelled in the knowledge that she was by far the youngest and most attractive of all the ladies who vied for the Captain's attention on their voyage to Bermuda. She had observed with disdain that some of the leather skinned oldies made their advances so obvious. How pathetic they were. As if the Captain could be even remotely interested in their shrivelled, worn out bodies. She hunkered down to avoid interaction with the plebs she was now forced to share a bed with.

Responding to a scrabbling and rustling noise Jenni addressed a shadowy figure. 'Come on out, what on earth do you think you are you doing there? A woman emerged from the furthest and darkest corner of the life raft. She was dressed in nondescript clothing, her hair completely covered by a hand crocheted pull on hat; she was still wearing dark glasses.

'Sorry . . . I . . . I'm just a bit frightened.'
'Oh it's you, Ms Sparrow, are you hurt?'

16

'No, just wet and uncomfortable.'

'Aren't we all,' another voice from the shadows grumbled.

'Oh yes, and you are?'

'It doesn't matter who I am, leave me alone.'

'I need to know your name for the record,' Jenni sounded annoyed.

'Oh just call me Jack.'

'Jack, what? I need to know it for the manifest,'

'You won't . . . Oh what does it matter now; it's Jack Brownlow, satisfied?'

'Thank you . . . Mr Brownlow.'

One of the last to be added to her list was undoubtedly the oldest person aboard and sat shivering in a corner. Jenni unfolded one of the foil blankets and covered the frail body as she asked the woman's name.

'Thank you,' she spoke quietly with an accent Jenni found hard to place. 'My name is Helena Philipa Papas.'

'Well, Helena you just rest there. This may be only thin but you will soon be feeling warmer.'

'Thank you my dear. Perhaps it might be appropriate at this moment for the priest, here to say a prayer for us all.'

Jenni took in the crumpled dark form of the last of her charges. 'Reverend Goodfellow isn't it?' she said, would you like to say a prayer for us?'

'Well perhaps a few words of comfort might help,' he replied. He offered a short prayer and in doing so reminded them all of the plight of the others on the ship some of whom may not have been lucky enough to make the safety of a raft.

'Thank you . . . Reverend most appropriate I'm sure.' Jenni said. Having completed the introductions, Jenni quickly assigned a two-hour lookout rota among the more able of the passengers and crew. 'Well, now we know who's who I think we should settle down and rest as much as possible. I'll turn the torch out now to save the batteries. All right?'

Chapter 2

The passengers did their best to make themselves comfortable in their damp clothing. Isolated on a gently undulating foggy void, many found comfort or escape in sleep. Others were not so lucky.

Night Talk

Despite being exhausted, some of the survivors were pumped so full of adrenalin they needed to sit up and talk. Their conversations hushed in deference to those who curled up and tried to sleep.

'Are you awake, young Tony?' David whispered.

'Yes . . . Can't sleep . . . too excited I suppose.'

'I hardly think excited is the appropriate word.'

'Oh I don't know, I was bored to death doing that waitering job.'

'So being drowned to death is better is it?'

'We won't drown, as long as we remain calm. Nice, cosy life-raft, plenty of provisions, we can sit here for days if we have to.'

'Do you really think so?'

'Yeah, no problem. Mind you, for a while there I did think my number was up.'

'When you were in the water?'

'Yes and before that too.'

'Why, what happened?'

'Well, having been demoted from waiting tables, I was working in freeway. That's the passage that runs the length of the ship, way below the passenger decks.

It gives access for the crew to all the hidden services onboard.

'I was pushing a trolley load of deserts from the cold room and just passing the laundry complex when there was this loud bang followed by a horrible grinding noise. The ship rocked violently to starboard then came back up again as it ground to a stop. I was pitched forward onto a tray-full of crème-caramel and the trolley skittered through the laundry entrance with me on it. I guess I must have caught my head on something and knocked myself out, because the next thing I remember was that I was lying on the floor in a pool of cold custard and syrup. The laundry boys, all little Philipinos, were slipping and sliding in the mess as they clambered over me to join the stampede for the exits.

It was like a stirred up ant's nest down there but with a Dolby soundtrack turned up full. People were screaming, crying, praying to all sorts of deities and everyone was telling everyone else what to do. Chaos, I can tell you. However, by the time I got my head together, the mob had gone. I kind of staggered out into freeway. It was silent as a Benedictine Monk's dinner party, except for the occasional groan from the ship's hull, like a giant with toothache. Then I began to hear the rush of water. Luckily, I was fairly well aft, because the first signs of flooding could be made out in the bow. Automatic doors were closing all along the corridor, red warning lights flashing over them.

'I made a run for the nearest companionway. By the time I reached the top, the ship was listing badly. At each turn, the flights were alternately almost flat or nearly vertical. My muster station was on the starboard side but when I got there, the lifeboats were already abandoned.

'Through the fog, I could see a few people bobbing about in the sea on that side but that was all. I clambered up onto one of the ship's boats, where I knew I could find an emergency tote bag. I grabbed it and was climbing down when the lifeboat shifted on its davits and momentarily crushed me against a stanchion. I fell against the hull and, being lubricated by custard, slid down the side of the ship into the sea. I swam as best I could, mostly leg only. I knew I had to get away before the ship sucked me down. From then on I didn't see a soul until you found me.'

'My God, Lad you are lucky to be alive.'

Tony cupped his hand round his watch to make out the luminous hands. 'Only one-thirty, God the night is dragging, who else is awake?'

Ken Watts had raided the bar before leaving the ship; a bottle of fine cognac was being passed around.

'Drink, Ted?'

David waggled the distinctive Courvoisier bottle out of the tent like flap.

'Thank you but I don't drink brandy. I once had a problem with it.

'Oh, Ok, all the more for us,' David took another long swig and passed the bottle back to Ken. He could see the lookout sporadically illuminated in the orange beacon fixed to the raft's canopy. 'What about you Ted, where were you when it happened?'

'In some ways it was a blessing.' said Ted, 'I was sitting next to this tedious rich American woman at dinner. You know the sort; blue rinse, gold everywhere, Hermes-scarf-and-blazer type. She's not here is she?' He squinted in through the hatch. 'Anyway, at one point I remember thinking that given the choice of her boring me to death or going down with a sinking ship, I would choose the latter.' Turney found he was expressing the sort of thoughts he would normally have kept to himself. 'People say you should be careful what you wish for, don't they.'

Ted realised he was babbling in an uncustomary way but felt the need to get the words out of his head as if that would right the situation.

'The bang took us all by surprise of course. There were a few jokes around the table about icebergs or the Captain not taking enough tonic with his gin. Then, as the china and silverware began sliding down the table, it reality hit us.

'There was no orderly procession to the muster station for this table. It was a mad dash, like racehorses out of the gate. You should have seen Mrs Blue Rinse move. She must have been eighty if she was a day but she was off like a steeple-chaser, jumping over chairs and people as she made for the stairs.' He gave an uneasy laugh. 'Some of us were far more restrained; I had to help an elderly couple make their way to the exit before taking care of myself. I saw others leading strangers by the hand towards the doors.

'By the time I got on deck, the ship was listing badly and I could see I was going to have to jump . . . like everyone else here, I suppose. It was surreal wasn't it . . . like being on a movie set. I kept thinking a director would shout 'cut' and we'd all go and have a cup of tea. Then someone shouted in my ear, 'In you go' and the next thing I knew I was in the water with everyone else.

'Strange how one's mind works, isn't it. My first thought was for Anna, my wife. Then I remembered she wasn't with me. I . . . I'm travelling on my own now. I must get used to that.'

Diana must have dozed for a while lulled by the sound of the gentle sea slurping, and lapping against the raft. The whiff of perfume, garlic, and rubber reminded her, of the dentist.

Looking around at all the people in the raft, she asked, 'Does anybody know what happened? I was getting ready for tonight's show when the ship started to shudder. Jasus, I thought this is it! Then that loud bang and scratching, clanking, metallic noise. What do you think was the cause of it, did we hit a submarine? I've heard of that happening.'

'No point in speculating. We can't know for sure, at this stage,' another Northern accent, from a dark corner replied, 'could be a reef . . . or . . . I'm sure we'll find out exactly what happened, when we get ashore.'

Diana squinted through the gloom to find out where the soft but authoritative voice came from. Her gaze settled on a tall, broad man with a receding grey hairline and neatly clipped moustache. He was sitting huddled under one of the foil sheets they had been issued with. His eyes were closed but she knew it was him that spoke out.

'Was that you who said that? You baldy, what's your name?'

Lazily lifting his eyelids and noticing Diana's stare he said, 'Me? I'm Ken. You're one of the entertainment crew . . . dancer . . . you're . . . Irish that's it. What part of Ireland are you from? I worked in Ireland for a while in the 70's. Tell me Miss . . .'

'Diana . . . Diana Somers,' she cautiously replied.

'Tell me, Diana, you don't happen to have a black balaclava in that suitcase of yours do you? Maybe a pipe bomb or something. You wouldn't happen to be Catholic would you? Yes, you were one of the last to board this raft I remember,' he laughed.

Several people on board giggled at his jibe.

'I see, let's have a joke at my expense, because I'm Irish; from Londonderry to be precise. That doesn't make me a terrorist; how dare you accuse me! Yes, I am Catholic, not that it's any of your bloody business. That's defamation of character that is. It's like saying that every Irish Catholic is a terrorist.' Diana shouted angrily, waking the few passengers who had managed to nod off.' Anyone else think that too? And while we're casting aspersions, why stop there?' She glared around at their shadowed faces. 'Don't you all want to know what's in my bag, I mean . . . I might be carrying a hand grenade or a knife . . . don't you want to search it?' Gesturing for him to look inside, she opened the bag so he could see. Go on have a good nose. 'Oh and by the way, what is your religion?'

'Of course I don't want to look inside your bag. Will you please close it? The sight of all your naughty undies is a big turn on, especially imagining you in them.'

'Don't you try that smooth line with me mister,' she said, trying hard not to smile. 'You're not getting out of it that easily. This is all some cheap jibe at me to make you look good. Well, answer my question? What is your religion?'

'No denomination, I despise organised religions. Those bigots are the cause of half the suffering in this world . . . Although for simplicity I put down Church of England why?'

'God damn it, what's happening?' a disgruntled voice hissed in the dark. 'Keep it down you two; some of us are trying to get some rest.'

Diana giggled, shuffled across the raft to get closer to her adversary and lowered her tone, 'Oh well say no more. The eternal religious debate, I've had it all my life. Please don't start on Henry the VIII. And Papal rule Leviticus, the Vatican, Catherine of Aragon and all that.' She knew she was gorgeous, particularly when her wild blue eyes got angry.

'Listen . . . Diana, sorry if I offended you. I was out of line. The last thing I want to do is rock the boat, sorry no pun intended. No seriously, I mean we're all going to be here for some time we've just got to get on with it . . . I'm Ken Watts by the way, I was a policeman during the troubles, but you're right, I had no right to say what I did . . . Am I forgiven?'

He did have a certain puppy dog appeal, she thought. *For his age, he looks distinguished and he had his own teeth.* She took his extended hand as he introduced himself.

'I loved to dance, when I was your age, but . . .' His voice trailed off and he closed his eyes again.

You may not be able to dance but you have dancing green eyes, Diana thought.

It was close to dawn by the time tiredness overcame them and the conversations petered out.

The sun was rapidly burning off the fog by the time the castaways stirred. One by one, they clambered to the hatches to tend to their bodily functions. Each one scanned the horizon in the hope of seeing a rescue ship steaming towards them. Always, they returned to their places silent and disappointed. In fact, there was nothing afloat on that turgid, grey sea. Not even another lifeboat. The sense of isolation was palpable. Despite the issue of food in the form of high calorie nutrient bars and a ration of bottled water, depression was setting in.

Conscious of her duty to keep morale up, Jenni drew her knees up to her, not unsubstantial, chest and racked her brains for ideas. She remembered the initial introductions, and how most people had seemed to want to say more, releasing outpourings of what were probably vastly embellished facts, perhaps in an effort to subdue their panic.

'Hey everyone', she called out, her Midland twang, jarring some from their maudlin reverie. 'How about if we tell some stories from our lives to pass the time and take our minds off this bloody predicament? I'll bet you all have an interesting tale or two to tell. In fact I'm sure we will be rescued long before everyone has had a turn.'

Turning her head to the right she spotted a gentleman, his face illuminated in the hazy morning light. He was peering into the empty seascape through the open hatchway. She hoped the anxiety she was feeling was not reflected in her voice as she asked, 'David, would you start us off? You look like an interesting sort of a bloke.'

Raft of Life

Chapter 3

Alone in a calm but seemingly vast and empty ocean, the little group of survivors agreed to pass the time by regaling each other of their past doings. D.J. Postlethwaite was up first.

The Entrepreneur's Tale

He looked round at his surroundings and shuddered. *How on earth can I survive this ordeal?* he thought. *I've got used to rich living; loads of comforts with people to do my bidding. It's years since I needed to just survive and live on my wits.* To add to his misery, he couldn't see his wife's life boat. He was worried and felt nauseous from travel sickness pills the bossy cruise director had insisted they took. The fog was getting thicker by the minute and he shivered in his wet clothes from having had to jump into the sea as the ship was sinking. He was jerked to reality as he realised someone was speaking to him.

'Sorry . . . What did you say? I'm so preoccupied with thoughts of my wife, she's been so ill. I wish we could still see the other boats.' He tried to withdraw from his reverie and concentrate on his life raft companions.

'We have to try to pass the time as pleasantly as possible,' Jenni repeated, 'though I'm sure it won't be too long before they find us. We were just wondering, as we introduced ourselves earlier, we could recount a story from our past to keep each other amused. It'll help to get to know each other a bit. Can we count you in?' An attractive, curvaceous, young blond was speaking with a hint of the Midlands in her voice. He recognized the Assistant Cruise Director, Jenni Carter.

'I suppose so . . . Would you like me to kick off?' he replied. *Might as well humour her,* he thought, *and it'll take my mind off things.* He looked round at the other survivors.

'That'd be good if you don't mind,' she replied.

'Some of you may have heard of me as I've antique shops and auction rooms, "Postlethwaite's." We're all over the northeast. I have had many other successful ventures as well. I'm a self made man. I was proud of that but recently my life has fallen apart. I don't mind telling you, I needed help.' His eyes misted over as he remembered recent events.

'Life was not good when I was a child. You can tell from my accent, I come from the North of England, near to Whitby. My father was a small hill farmer. He was a hard man for whom I had little affection. He just scraped a living. As you may be able to imagine, we had few home comforts and the food was very basic most of the time. My mother tried to make up for the deficiencies in our way of life by giving us loads of affection; that is when my father wasn't looking. I am one of three; I have a younger brother and sister. I seemed to be my mother's favourite, being the first born, which helped me to cope with the beatings I endured regularly from my father for some minor misdemeanour or other. As soon as we could walk, we had to do tasks around the home and then the farm. Dad made it clear we all had to work to pay our way. As he put it, "I want no free loaders round 'ere." We didn't really have a childhood. We had to grow up quickly.

'Mother was a good woman. She performed all the usual duties of a farmer's wife, keeping chickens, selling eggs, making bread but in addition she also did cleaning at a big house a mile away. It brought in a bit of extra cash when there was little to be had from the farm.

'What kind of farm was it?' Ken asked.

'Dad mainly kept sheep, so if lambing wasn't as successful as he hoped or the price of lamb dropped, then we had to rely on mother's earnings, meagre as they were.

'The house was cold and draughty with no double glazing or anything. I don't remember if it ever had any improvements made. We could see our breath hang in the air in the winter. The fire gave out little warmth into the room; you had to be on top of it to really feel its heat. When Dad was around, he tended to hog it, so the rest of us wore many layers of clothes and kicked a ball around in the yard to keep warm.

'Sometimes Mother brought back clothes from the big house. The owners had children who were not too dissimilar in age to us and the lady of the house sent us their hand me downs. I resented this more than I can tell you. I wanted my own clothes. Those bought just for me at the shops in Scarborough or Middlesbrough. No such luck.

'It was a rare occasion for there to be meat on the table, so new clothes were never on the cards. I saw the people from the big house as upper crust twits who patronised us. I swore to myself that I would get my revenge on them. The thought ate at me. I imagined that they the treated my mother badly whilst she was doing their menial tasks, though she would hear none of it. Mine was an unreasoning hate.'

'What were they called?' Ken asked.

'Does it matter?'

'Well . . .'

'If you must know, this family were the Hunter-Smyths: the father was a stockbroker and he was obviously very good at what he did. I bet they had meat on the table every day.'

'Did I hear you say, "Hunter-Smyths"' Ken interrupted, 'only I recall a case . . .'

'Their house,' David went on, ignoring the interruption, 'was centrally heated with double glazing and thick carpets, no expense spared. They didn't have to put buckets under drips because they couldn't afford to have the roof mended or go down the yard to an earth closet. Their lives were so dissimilar to ours that we had nothing in common. I seethed inside at the injustice that had made the gap in our standard of living such poles apart. I went to the local village school, whereas their son Jeremy went to a posh prep school in York and would go on to a public school.'

'Yes, met that sort,' Isobel murmured.

'He would mix with other upper crust twits and form friendships which would help him in business or whatever else he decided to do. I decided then that I would have to change what the future held for me and not perpetuate the situation in which my parents were imprisoned.'

'Good for you,'

'I worked so hard at school that I was considered a swot.' David went on, 'It didn't endear me to my classmates who were happy to coast along and go out to play in the evenings. There was a small school library and the library service brought books to the village every month that I could borrow. I read all the books that I could lay my hands on.

'My teachers too saw that I thirsted for knowledge and would sometimes lend me their books. It wasn't easy to find the time to read, as I had to work on the farm after school and help my father. I snatched time when my parents thought I'd gone to sleep. I had a stash of candles I used so I didn't waste the precious paraffin. It was rationed like everything else. Nothing was going to stop me. I would get to the Grammar School somehow. With a blanket wrapped round me, I would study by the flickering light. My diligence paid off. I did pass the eleven plus. I felt such elation.

'My father gave me no encouragement though. He growled that nothing good would come of it and he wasn't going to pay for fancy new uniforms. My mother took me to one side and told me not to worry as she'd managed to put some of her cleaning money away to buy a uniform for me. It wouldn't be new: she'd been in touch with the school to find out about second hand stuff and they had a nearly new sale just before the beginning of term. It seemed that I wasn't the only one who couldn't afford to have new clothes. That thought did help.

'I persuaded the landlord in the local pub to let me work washing glasses to get some money and then I progressed to helping in the cellar. I kept to the background so no one knew I was working and objected to my being too young. By that time I could pass for much older anyway as I was a big lad with large muscles from the heavy work I did at home. My father objected to my doing this too, so I had to redouble efforts at home to make sure that I didn't get yet another beating. They weren't as frequent by this time, as my size now posed a threat to his physical supremacy. He vented his frustration on mother and my siblings. I tried to diffuse the situation by giving her half of all I earned. Not that it was a princely sum, but it did ease things for her. However, I often heard her defending me and this led to more rows between them. These often became brutally violent but my muscular dominance eventually prevented that, at least in my presence.

'One time, I saw Jeremy Hunter-Smyth in the school holidays and seethed with hate. He'd never done me any harm but the differences in our family situations made me bitter with resentment. He'd joined the village junior cricket team and played with them to great effect in the holidays. He was a great batsman and a brilliant bowler. They depended on him and looked forward to his holidays. Perhaps I would have been good at cricket too if I'd been given the chance. I had to work, so there was no chance of my finding out. It just added to my feeling of injustice . . . jealousy I suppose, and to my hatred of Jeremy. The rage I felt at times had to be worked off, so the heavy work, the demands of the farm proved to be a form of release. Fencing, manhandling sheep into the dip or wrestling with them to shear or clip their hooves helped. I think it gave me extra strength, so perhaps it had a positive side as well as a negative one. I also developed academically; my reports from the Grammar School were exemplary. My way up the ladder had started. I was going to get somewhere in the world!

'As I got older I was able to get better jobs in Whitby where the school was located. It brought in more money and I saved hard. I loved looking in the antique shop windows and seeing all the beautiful objets-d'art. In time, I got a job working in the sale-rooms. Sometimes, when there was a specialist sale, the items were fabulous. I handled them carefully, with a reverence even. I loved the quality. I couldn't learn enough from Kit, the head porter. He'd worked for the auctioneer for years and what he didn't know wasn't worth knowing. The auctioneer, James Grayson, was an elderly man and saw how appreciative I was of the items he was selling as well as my ambition to progress. He took me under his wing. I loved being in that environment. I felt as though I had found a home. I felt excitement as a new consignment came in. What treasures would it contain?

'It caused many a fight with my father who wanted me to work for him. His strength was diminishing due to the hard life he'd lived. I realise now that he saw me as essential to keep the farm going. He'd never known any different. But he'd made his choices and I had to be able to make mine.

'"Let the lad alone," my mother would say, "E'll make something of 'isel. Don't 'old 'im back. George is more like a farmer, 'e's doing a good job. Emily is 'elping me in the 'ouse and with the chickens. She's a good baker and with the money our David gives me, we're able to buy the ingredients for 'er to make the cakes she's selling in the village. She's getting a lot of orders. So things are getting better without our David going into the farm. Let 'im be. He won't forget us. 'asn't 'e allus given me what 'e can and 'e's worked 'ard for you in the past."

'"Aye," I heard him growl in reply, "unless 'e gets too big for 'is boots with 'is big ideas. You've allus been soft on 'im. You watch 'im. 'E'll soon forget the likes of us who raised 'im. 'E sees 'issel' as better than us. Just listen to the way 'e talks now. 'E looks down on us already."

'Did they really talk like that,' Franny asked shyly, 'with the accent and all?'

'Oh aye, we all did back then.' David replied, 'Anyway . . . I was due to take my 'O' levels. My father had already warned me that I had to leave school and take a "proper" job.

'"You'll 'ave t' get a man's job and stop all this book learning," he said, "All these fancy ideas of yours to be a cut above all the folks round 'ere are no good. The likes of us don't get breaks we 'ave t' make do. The sooner you realize that the better. Stop looking down your neb at us or you're not too big for me t' gie you a good 'idin."

'I made him aware very graphically what I would do if he tried. By that time, I was six feet tall and well built, so could easily overpower him. I pinned him to the wall and raised my fist to knock him to the floor. I didn't follow through as my mother pulled at my arm and pleaded for me to stop. I just dropped him and walked away. It hardened my resolve to get away.

'My grades at 'O' level were excellent. I went to see Mr Grayson and put it to him that I had to leave school and wanted to become a trainee auctioneer. I wanted to know all he knew.

'I put a proposition to him, "You know how hard I've worked part-time but now I want to work for you full-time," I said, "I can make your life easier in the future if you allow me to do this. I'll do any exams by correspondence course so I don't have to take time off. I'll work my socks off for you; however, I do need to live here. I know there's a disused flat above the sale-room. It's a bit dilapidated but I can make it nice over time. You can take the rent from my salary. It'll mean that the security of the premises will be strengthened. I know you've been worried about the possibility of break-ins. I'll be a credit to you and earn my wage," I pleaded.

'"Well lad, I can't deny that you're a good worker and very committed to learning all you can. Kit has commented that he's never had such a good helper on the floor. He loves telling you all about the items we're selling too as you are so keen. I'll have to think about it. I'll let you know in a couple of days," he replied smiling.

'I was on tenterhooks until he called me in when I went to work two days later.

'"Now then, I've given due consideration to all that you said, and it's not without its difficulties, but this is what I've decided."

'He went on to say that he needed a junior auctioneer to take some of the responsibility off him. He felt he needed to take some time off now and then as he now was feeling his age. I believe he was sixty-five at the time. He hadn't anyone to follow him as his only child, a daughter, wanted to be an interior designer. He would employ me full-time but he would give me a low wage to start and throw in the flat free of charge, as it needed fitting up. If I proved my worth during the next year and brought in more revenue then he'd increase my salary.

'I was overjoyed. I now had a foothold on the ladder of success and could leave the farm behind. I resolved to work all the hours there were. I enrolled in a course at the polytechnic and showed him I meant what I said. I hoped it'd show my brother and sister that you could get out of a rut and give them ideas of how to better themselves. My mother cried but was pleased for me.

'My father? Well his response was what I expected. "It'll all come to no good, I warn you. You can't come back 'ere when it doesn't work out. You've made your bed and now you can lie in it." He was angry, not pleased for me at all.

'From time to time I saw my archenemy, Jeremy, at the auction with his mother as she bid for more nice things with which to embellish her house. The hair bristled on the back of my neck each time I saw him. He always raised a hand in greeting which I didn't return.

'I worked hard and soon managed to get the flat habitable. I bought a few basic things at the auction so I didn't have to part with too much cash. It was soon as clean as a new pin and I kept it like that. There was nothing that was too much trouble for me. I suggested that new advertisements were placed in the press, not just the local ones but those magazines that the County Set read. Mr Grayson saw the advantage of this so it was done. It did raise our profile and more punters came from far and wide to buy. We sent out more and more brochures of our specialist sales. The money came in much more readily, which helped me justify my position. I got a raise and soon it became a regular thing.

'I was talking to Mr Grayson one day and he mentioned that his daughter had got a young man.

'"Who might that be?" I asked. I really fancied her myself and was trying to pluck up courage to ask her out when she was next in Whitby.

'"Jeremy Hunter Smyth. She met him in Leeds where they're both working. It's not been going on long but they seem to hit it off," he remarked casually.

'I saw red. Not him again. I just couldn't be rid of him. Now he was muscling in on my girl. How could I compete? I'd saved up a bit of cash and so I decided it was time to splash a bit of it about; I'd buy a car. I couldn't let him have it all his own way. I made my play when she came up at the weekend. To my surprise, she agreed to go out with me for lunch at one of the country pubs. The Wheat Sheaf I think it was. We really did enjoy ourselves. She was funny and, to my utter amazement, interested in all I said and did. I suggested casually, that we would be a good partnership in business as I could find all the lovely things she needed to furnish the gorgeous rooms she designed. Now that I was mobile, I could go round other sale-rooms and find things on my day off. Other auctioneers would let me know when certain items were coming up that may be of interest to her. She seemed to find it appealing and said she would let me know. I set my stall out after that to sweep her off her feet.

'I kept wondering if she was still seeing Jeremy. It was eating at me. I was insanely jealous but knew I couldn't show it.

'"Have you seen Jeremy Hunter-Smyth recently? I think he works not far from you Leeds," I enquired in what I hoped was a nonchalant manner.

'"Why? Do you know him?" she asked.

'"Oh, he comes from the same village as me; I just thought you may have run into him. He seems to get everywhere. He's often in the sale-room." I looked at my nails to disguise my intense interest in the reply.

'"I did see him a couple of times but haven't for a while. I know he bought a flat in Leeds so he must be getting things for it. Things are cheaper in Whitby than over there," she replied without guile.

'I felt a lot better. I proceeded to court her when work allowed. I was getting quite fond of her. Then her old man called me into his office. He told me that he had to make life easier for himself as he'd developed heart trouble and the doctor had warned him about the busy schedule he'd been keeping. It seemed to him that now he should hand over some of the responsibility to someone younger, he explained.

'I hardly dare hope what that may mean for me. He went on to say that as I'd shown commitment, hard work and loyalty to him then he would return it.

'"What I'm saying, is that it's time for me to start handing things over to you. In time we could come to some arrangement for you to take over the business altogether. Mind you you'd need to invest some cash in it," he explained. He stopped and rubbed his fingers together for a moment before going on.

'"Mind you, if our lass and you were to wed then that would be different. She's my only child. In that case, I just might make the business over to you both. You'd be partners. You'd be the one with the expertise and run it but she would have a say as well as an income from it in her own right." He looked at me through narrowed eyes as though examining a specimen.

'I couldn't believe what I was hearing. I must have looked stunned. Eventually I said, "Well it depends on what your Grace wants doesn't it? Have you spoken to her?"

'"Yes, I have. She seems quite happy with the idea. I thought for a while that she might make it with Jeremy but she seems more taken with you. I believe she thinks you are her soul mate," he responded.

'I couldn't take it in. Eventually I heard myself stammer, "Well if Grace is happy with it then so am I. I enjoy being with her. We share hopes for the future."

'"You'd better get your skates on then and ask her then hadn't you. Do it right mind! If you ever treat her badly I'll kill you," he said menacingly. I believed he meant it. I was sure that if he couldn't do it himself he'd have someone else to do it for him.

'We did marry and though I can't say I loved her then, I did appreciate her. For so long, I'd been so focused on getting on; I had forgotten what it meant. If ever I had known that is. There hadn't been much of it in my parent's house. Our business ventures were very successful and in time, we had two lovely children that I was passionate about. This surprised me. I vowed that they would have all the benefits I'd seen the Hunter-Smyths enjoy. He still was the major object of my hate and I didn't pass up any opportunity of doing him a disservice. I started a whispering campaign against him and his company at the gentleman's club I joined in Leeds. If he wanted an item in the sale-room, I made sure he didn't get it if I could. That is until an event happened recently.

'We now live in a good part of York as well as having a pad in London. During a visit to her old man in Whitby; we went for a relaxing walk along the quay when some loud mouthed youths barged between us knocking my wife flying. She ended up in the harbour! I couldn't swim and the shock had knocked the breath out of her. In horror, I reached for a lifebelt as I saw a man streak past me and dive in to get her. When I peered over the edge of the quay, I realised that it was Jeremy Hunter-Smyth! For once, I was relieved to see him. He too was visiting his parents. Thank God for that!

'Some men had gone down some steps nearby and had hauled her lifeless, dripping body up onto the quay by the time I could get her there. Others had rung the ambulance, another was a first aider who immediately sprang into action, he gave her the kiss of life and CPR until the ambulance arrived. I felt useless. I was shivering with shock and someone handed me a blanket and helped me into the ambulance so I could accompany her to Whitby Cottage hospital.

'She was quickly being worked on by the medics at the hospital. Thank goodness, it wasn't far away. However, they did decide that she needed more intensive care than was available there. She had lost consciousness.

"'It's just a precaution but she'll have to be transferred to the main regional hospital that has more facilities. Try not to worry too much," the doctor explained. However, his furrowed brow made me realise it was serious.

'I was in bits. "I can't lose her. She and the kids are my life." It suddenly hit me as I followed the ambulance to Scarborough. "God I really do love her and can't live without her!" It was a revelation.

"'Things are going to be very different from now on," I vowed. "I can't even hate Jeremy now." I was stunned. Perhaps I had been wrong all these years. Me, the great self made man had perhaps been mistaken! The thought rocked my foundations. It was one of the pillars on which I'd built my life. How could I go on? My introspection was interrupted by our arrival at Scarborough Hospital.

'The paramedics sprang into action. My wife was swiftly taken into the inside. The next hour or so was bewildering. I was redundant. For once, I couldn't fix things. When Grace was installed in the intensive care unit, they sent for me. She had tubes everywhere. The smell of antiseptic was pervasive, as each visitor had to scrub their hands with it. They informed me that things were grave. She'd sustained a head injury that was causing great concern. Swelling was a potential problem and only time would tell. Patience was the name of the game. She must have hit her head on a rock when she entered the water. For forty eight hours, she hung between life and death. I prayed like never before. God hadn't helped me much during my childhood so I'd never had time for Him. Now, all of a sudden, it was the one thing I could do. The hospital chaplain came to see me and I must say I did find his company re-assuring.

'Grace fortunately, though ill, did come through the 48 hours and the dreaded swelling was contained. It eventually shrank back to normal without necessitating invasive surgery.

'I'd had spent hours at her bedside white with anxiety. At times, he I wept for the lost opportunities to make her feel cherished.

'My sister Emily brought our children in to see their mother as soon as she was out of danger and on the ward. I was greeting them enthusiastically, when I became aware of another figure hovering in the background.

'Emily saw me stare and looked round at him then turned to addressed me, "David . . . Jeremy wondered how Grace was progressing. He's rung me every day for information. We also have some news for the two of you. We've been seeing each other for a while now. We love each other. In fact, we can't do without each other. We're going to get married. It's important to us that you give us your blessing."

'She paused expectantly. I was stunned. I hadn't even known they'd been dating. Emily now worked as a chef in Leeds, having passed with flying colours her catering exams and had made a name for herself.

'I gathered myself together. This was the man who had saved my wife's life. Now he was rocking my life in another way. I wasn't in a position to deny him anything.

'I recovered after a moment, putting out my hand and thanked him profusely.

"Jeremy, I'm so indebted to you. No thanks can ever express my gratitude. Now it seems you are to be part of my family. Welcome!"

'My stomach was doing cartwheels and I shivered. I was struggling to process all the changes in our circumstances. Little did he know how much I owed him. I would have to spend the rest of my days trying to make up for all the mean things I had done to him over the years. It just shows how wrong you can be about a person; also that your thinking can be very warped by life experiences. Revenge was no longer the name of the game. It's recompense and forgiveness.

'I've a long way to go yet in terms of developing a new philosophy for my life, but I've made a start. Now that I know I'm fallible, it's given me much more humility. We came on this cruise to help my wife to regain her strength and for me to show her how much I love her. I've let her down a lot in the past on that score. I can't lose her now. I wish we could see the other boats.

'What are our and their chances of being rescued? Tell me honestly.'

'If she made it onto one of the lifeboats, she'll be fine,' Jenni replied. 'They're equipped with GPS transponders and no doubt the coastguard will be already on its way to pick them up.'

'I always thought the well off had it made, but perhaps not.' David buried his head in his hands.

'Don't be so hard on yourself. We all make mistakes,' the voice of Tony Mc Bride broke in.

'What about our and their chances of being rescued? Do we have this GPS thing?

'We have a transponder that the search aircraft can pick up,' Jenni responded, 'but it does not have a global positioning satellite transmitter, takes too much power, they have to be in line of sight to pick it up so for us it may take a little longer, that's all.'

'It must be better now the fog has cleared, don't you think?' DJ looked around the company for answers. 'I saw my wife get into the last lifeboat to leave but I was on the next deck up. I won't be happy until I see her again.'

'Don't worry, David,' said Tony, 'the US Coastguard know roughly where we are so we're bound to see their planes coming overhead soon. It won't be long before we're spotted. Your wife will be in a better off situation than we are. At least she wasn't wet when she abandoned ship. Those lifeboats are better equipped than this raft. She'll be fine. I'm sure she'll be waiting for you when you step ashore.'

Jenni Carter broke in, 'Thanks D.J. I'm sure Tony's right. Now, who wants to go next?' She looked expectantly at the rest of her charges.

Chapter 4

Eyes turned to the old woman with the pleasantly plump figure who shuffled into a more upright position; she seemed to want to get something off her chest.

The Teacher's Tale

The woman in the red dress cleared her throat, eyes turned towards her as she spoke.

'I just knew this would happen. The very first cruise I've ever taken. I should have trusted my instincts and gone on a nice, safe package holiday to Majorca! I always vowed that I'd never go on a voyage, as I've always been terrified of boats. Why, you might ask? Well, when I was about five years old, my father had the brilliant idea of taking us all on a trip on a tug to escort one of those massive cruise liners out of the harbour. I have never forgotten the sight of that towering vessel so high above me. I felt sure that our tiny boat would be sucked right underneath. I think, there and then, I decided that travel by sea would never be an option for me and up until now, I have stuck to my decision.

'So what made you change your mind?'Jenni asked.

'Well, last year I retired and I made a list of five things to do before you die and this was one of them. I suppose I decided that it was time and, at last, I certainly would have the time to face my fears. I've never really done much travelling, although my husband and I did have a couple of holidays abroad. I was attracted to the idea of sailing into the Bermuda Triangle – I've always been intrigued by all those mysterious disappearances, you know! Well, I hope we're not just going to vanish into thin air! Maybe we'll be rescued by aliens!

'At least I've managed to cross two items off my list and, I suppose in all reality, I did actually go on a cruise, even if it was rather shorter than I planned. Strangely, I was just beginning to relax and enjoy myself. I'd got all dressed up in my new dress, lovely colour isn't it? Even though it's now quite ruined, and was looking forward to chatting with the people at my table. Then that awful fog surrounded us and I had a sort of premonition that something dreadful was going to happen. I gave myself a stern talking to about being more positive and optimistic and made my way to the bar for a drink or two before dinner. Then that bang! In my panic, I quite forgot what I was supposed to do, so I followed my instincts and made for the nearest exit. Even so, soon the ship was beginning to list and all I could think was, "Oh God, I'm going to die!" I never thought I'd make it to this liferaft. The water was so cold, I kept being dragged down by my dress and I kept swallowing water and choking. Just look at it now, what a waste.

'Come on now,' Jenni spoke gently to the distraught woman, 'Calm down, you're safe here. Why don't you tell us about the other things you wanted to do before you . . .'

'Yes, well, enough of that! What were the other four things? Well, I've never been an adventurous or confident person. Bit of a scaredy-cat really. I've never rebelled or questioned the fact that other people usually know better. So, you could say that this is my way of proving them all wrong. I've always behaved conventionally – nice, safe teaching job, nice, safe marriage, and nice, safe home! Boring you might say, but secure! These "twilight years" are probably my last chance to be bold, to "have a go!" Not for one moment did I ever anticipate ending up in such a dangerous situation though. I mean, what if there are sharks around or we run out of food before we are rescued?'

'Don't be silly! There are no sharks in these waters' Diana said without conviction, 'Are there?'

'They won't bother us,' Tony said reassuringly.

'Oh really . . . and I suppose there are some supplies on board? Well, yes, of course there are! I have to admit that I'm beginning to regret making that wretched list. Maybe I was tempting fate. Anyway, number one was to visit my friend in Australia, number two, travel to New York. This is number three – so I don't have much confidence in four or five – a safari and a tour of North Africa.'

'Why don't you tell us about Australia?' Jenni tried to encourage her.

'My best friend, Pat, immigrated to Australia the same year I married Ethan. Actually, she was supposed to get married on the same day as me but her fiancé changed his mind. I think she's rather glad about that now but at the time, she was devastated. Isn't it funny how sometimes, things happen for a reason? They'd bought a house, strangely enough, in the same village where I've always lived. No, I've never even moved away from the place where I was born, believe it or not. Well, I did mention I was a rather boring person.

'She used to come back to England regularly, but now both her parents are dead, there's no real need for those rather expensive visits. What an opportunity for me to realise one of my dreams, to go and see Australia for myself – something I'd been longing to do ever since she first went there! Just imagine actually being in Sydney, seeing that amazing Opera House and the wonderful bridge for myself, instead of watching it on the television! Actually walking on Bondi Beach with all those hunky surfers and maybe even seeing kangaroos, kookaburras and koalas in the Bush or wherever! I just couldn't wait to board that plane, I can tell you.'

'Oh, so you're not scared of flying then?'

'No, fortunately I'm not frightened of flying – just the opposite. From the moment I reach the airport, the excitement builds. Once I've checked in successfully, after all there's always a chance that there's been a mistake with my reservation, I feel so relaxed and happy. A bit of duty free shopping, a couple of drinks then it's off on the big, silver bird as Ethan used to say. But this time it was different. No Ethan! We split up two years ago, just drifted apart really, lived separate lives for years . . . I'd never travelled alone before and it is such a long way to Australia. I remember my feeling of absolute horror when I realised that I would have to change planes at Dubai. So many things could go disastrously wrong and, knowing my luck, they would.'

'What a surprise,' Ken muttered sarcastically.

'Well, guess who was stranded at Dubai Airport? Yes, it could only happen to me! That flipping plane sat on the tarmac at Birmingham Airport for over an hour, revving up or whatever it is they call it! We were an hour late taking off and, consequently, those of us who were travelling on to Sydney missed the connecting flight. What a surreal experience that turned out to be. Actually, the ground staff did their best to rush us through security to the gate but when we finally arrived there, even though people were still boarding, we weren't allowed on because the airline had very kindly arranged to have our bags off-loaded! You can just imagine how I felt! It was two o'clock in the morning, I was knackered and more than a mite upset, I can tell you! Having said that, things turned out rather better than I'd dared hoped for. The airline put on a minibus to a really posh hotel where I had a fabulous bedroom. I was even allowed to smoke inside the hotel. Naturally, I was too scared to sleep, in case I missed the next flight, but I did have a most interesting and extensive breakfast. What weird things they eat out there! I suppose they have to cater for international tastes but no bacon. That buffet must have had every kind of bread, fruit and eggs, but no bacon! Really!

'The next morning, well more like a few hours later, we were back at the airport. In a way, it was a shame we didn't get to see the sights of Dubai but at least I can say I've been there. Anyway, after a marathon journey of fourteen hours, the plane at last landed on Australian tarmac. Yay! I arrived in Sydney about five pounds heavier than when I set off. Well, they feed you constantly on these long-haul flights, stops you from going mad if you're eating, you know. Anyway, there I was at six o'clock in the morning thinking the worst was behind me. Wrong!'

'What could possibly have gone wrong at the airport?' Diana asked

'Well, while you're still on the plane, you have to fill out a form, declaring that you're not carrying any illegal substances and that apparently includes any edible goods. A friend had given me a necklace made from nuts and seeds that she'd bought for me in Cuba. So I declared that, just in case, but I didn't declare my cigarettes because the cashier in the duty-free at Birmingham Airport had told me I was allowed to take in four hundred. How was I supposed to know that actually, you're only allowed two hundred and fifty? Not a crime, surely? Apparently, yes!'

'Don't tell me,' Ken said in a bored tone, 'you were arrested.'

'Sort of,' Isobel ignored his sarcastic tone although it was beginning to annoy her. 'A very serious-looking customs officer emptied my hand luggage onto his table and stared at me most accusingly. You would have thought he'd just discovered a kilo of heroin in my bodysuit. "No officer, that's all me." You can all see how healthy my appetite is. I was hauled off before the judge, actually a more senior officer and informed that the import duty would be five times the value of the booty "I didn't know, officer." I quavered, doing my best to look like a sweet, innocent English lady. And to my amazement, he let me keep all my cigarettes without having to pay anything at all. Mind you, after such a horrendous journey, I probably did look as though I'd collapse at any moment. Maybe he was worried that I'd snuff it there and then. So at last, I was free to leave the airport and start enjoying myself, after a good night's sleep of course. Wrong! Trish's daughter lives in Sydney and was waiting for me. Fortunately, I'd been able to phone her from the hotel in Dubai, otherwise she would have been waiting all night. She drove me to the hotel and then took me on a nice, long walk down to the beach. Then, as she had to get to work, she left me 'to relax and enjoy myself. So, I found a café and had a much-needed cup of tea. It was quite surreal sitting there, looking at the sea and sky and thinking; *I really am on the other side of the world.* But I was so tired and I had to find my way back to the hotel – joke! All I could remember was that it was up a hill but nearly all the streets led up the hill. Eventually, after asking loads of people I found it, crawled into my room and slept.

The next day, I took a bus into the city and asked the driver to tell me when we arrived at the harbour. About half an hour later, the bus stopped and everybody got off. I looked round expectantly but there was no sign of the famous bridge at all. *It's happened again,* I thought. Taking a deep breath, I stood up, walked to the front of the bus and asked the driver where the harbour was. 'Round the corner,' he replied. And it was, along with the fantastic Opera house and all the ferries scurrying to and fro. I never realised how massive the harbour actually is. It opens out into a huge bay and the city itself is spread out all around. What an amazing sight that was. I don't think I've ever before taken so many great photographs or asked so many people if they'd mind taking photos of me. I suppose it gave me a bit of a pang to realise I was on holiday alone but was an exciting place to be alone in! I spent the day there and actually managed to find the bus back. That evening, Trish arrived, so I wasn't alone any more.

'We stayed in Sydney for another two days, during which she took me to the Sea World Centre. I don't really like fishy things, but there was a very intriguing seal-type creature called a dugong. It was all by itself in a tank because *he* had been a bit naughty with the female dugong! I felt really sorry for him but the keeper told us that he would be back in the main tank soon. Apparently, these creatures are the basis for the legends of mermaids. The sailors who saw them thought they were half fish, half females and that's how the stories started. You didn't know that, did you?'

'Well, I did actually.' Ken muttered.

'Anyway, my last night was spent inside the Opera House, seeing the ballet version of "The Merry Widow", it was fabulous. The music, the dancing and the costumes were out of this world and coincidently, both Trish and I could recall our mothers humming the waltz to us when we were young. When we came out, there in front of us were all the lights of Sydney Harbour. A sight I will never forget. My journey had certainly been worthwhile. The rest of my visit was spent at Trish's home in the Northern Rivers where we went walking, canoeing and exploring the small towns. There were times when I sat in her garden, having a cigarette, listening to the kookaburras and admiring the blossoming landscape. I couldn't believe that at last, I'd flown thousands of miles to be there. I was so proud of myself but I don't think I'll be doing it again. Well, unless we're rescued, I won't be doing anything again, will I?'

'Don't worry, Isobel, you'll soon be able to carry on fulfilling your bucket list,' Tony reassured her. 'Seeing as how you were so bored with this nice lady's story, Ken, why don't you tell us about your exciting life, as a policeman, was it?' the waiter feigned an exaggerated yawn.

Raft of Life

Chapter 5

Time passed slowly on the raft. The changeover of shifts on lookout, the periodic issue of food and a meagre ration of fresh water were all that marked the passage of time. With clear skies, the sun beat down on the turgid sea, scorching those who ventured outside and heating the canvas cover. However, with all the flaps open, a cooling current of air ventilated the reclining bodies enough to make it tolerable.

The Policeman's Tale

Ken Watts shifted his large, languid form to rest his bare back against the hot canvas side of the rafts tent-like cover. He allowed his olive green eyes to sweep the scattered survivors in the enclosure registering that the only one missing was Adam Stone, who was outside in the sun, no doubt diligently sweeping the horizon for a sign of rescue. Most of those around him had abandoned their foil blankets, as the day's heat built up, and were in various stages of undress.

'Yes,' he said at length, 'I was a policeman of sorts; started out as a cadet for the Greater Manchester Constabulary. Did pretty well too. Sheer hard work fast-tracked me to detective and youthful ambition drove me to seek more. So when Special Branch were looking for officers with Irish background for undercover work I jumped at the chance.' He shot a glance at Diana, who had been leaning against his shoulder and now pulled back to stare quizzically at him. 'That's right, Diana, I come from a long line of Irish Catholics. My grandparents came over to Liverpool before the First World War; my mother married a lad from Manchester and went back there with him to raise us kids. I was the eldest of four.' He smiled down at her, she scowled back and was about to say something when he held a finger to her lips, 'All will become clear,' he murmured. Then, louder, he addressed the company. 'But let me tell you about my time in Special Branch . . . if you're interested?' There was a ripple of consenting response so he went on.

'After a period of extra training, during which I resurrected my Irish heritage, in particular my Catholic upbringing, lapsed by then. Enough of the basics had become embedded for me to pass as reasonably devout. I grew a moustache,' he stroked the luxuriant, grey growth on his upper lip, 'and it was easy to put on the Scouse-Irish accent of my mother. I'd never get away with trying for an Ulster drawl but Liverpool was fine with the IRA. To cut a long story short, I was sent over to Armagh on an undercover mission to gather intelligence. It was in the mid eighties. Eighty-six, I think. Maggie Thatcher was Prime Minister at the time and there was word that they were planning another assassination attempt.' He smiled wryly. 'You remember the Brighton bomb, the Grand Hotel? They nearly got her that time. Although the attempt was unsuccessful in its primary aim, it did go as planned. This was something more direct. I found out about it but couldn't get the info out. I'd fallen under suspicion with the Commander I had attached myself to and suspicion was enough to get you killed in those days. I was lucky. The job was called off but the pall of suspicion still hung over me. That was just a week before Enniskillen. The bomb went off by a Cenotaph, which was at the heart of the parade. It was one of the IRA's biggest failures, as it was not aimed at killing civilians. Eleven people, ten civilians including a pregnant woman plus a police officer, were killed and 63 were injured. The IRA said it had made a mistake and that its target had been the British soldiers parading to the memorial. Our unit who carried out the bombing was disbanded. Loyalist paramilitaries responded to the bombing with revenge attacks on Catholic civilians in the Enniskillen area and the rest of the north. I was under threat from both sides so I decided to bug out, as the military say. I told them my mother was sick and I had to go back to Liverpool. They may be merciless killers but they love their mothers, so they let me go. In their eyes, it put me further from the chain of command but as a sympathiser and activist, I could still be of some use to them in England.

'I was glad to be back, the sectarian violence in Northern Ireland sickened me, I understood the political agenda but the way the sides were drawn up on either side of the religious divide and the stirring up that the clergymen on both sides did turned me against all forms of organised religion. A position I still hold today. More so, with the way Islam is being manipulated to justify such atrocities and repression nowadays. Don't get me wrong, I'm not an atheist; agnostic maybe. but there's still too many mysteries to rule out a supreme being in my opinion. I don't object to people having a faith, it's the misuse the factions use to influence the masses that upset me. At least back then, the IRA made some attempt to achieve a form of peace even if it had to be on their own terms. Who knows what will satisfy the radical fanatics our boys face now. Nothing short of world domination, I suppose.

'But I digress . . . Back in England I was stood down from Special Branch and returned to Greater Manchester Police. I'd gone in as a Detective Constable and four years later returned as an Inspector. On traffic, would you believe? So boring after what I'd been through, but it was the only opening for my rank. At least it was regular hours and it gave me a chance to meet and marry my Dervla. We settled down and she was soon with child. But I longed for some action.

'I did get back into crime eventually and through the underworld, my colleagues and I had to deal with, I discovered another IRA connection and told my former bosses in the anti terrorist squad. They co-opted me again. The trail led south, well Manchester was not on their target list or so we thought.

'I followed up a contact in Kilburn, London. Got myself into the right place at the right time and although I didn't know the target, they gave me the job of driving a truck into the City of London. It was what we used to call a *co-op* bomb because all the ingredients were readily available to the public. It was the biggest one ever deployed in London. At that time, the Provo's policy was to attack only military and economic targets. My instructions were to park outside the Stock Exchange, if it could be put out of action, the damage to the British economy would be devastating. Unfortunately, I was not familiar with that part of London, so I asked the way and was misdirected by some idiot to a building called the Baltic Exchange.

'Fuelled by adrenalin, I still arrived ahead of the allotted time. I locked the van up and scooted away as quickly as I could. Meanwhile a warning was put in to the authorities but the evacuation and security cordon was thrown around the wrong place. At the end of the road I looked back to see a panda car pull up alongside the van. These were coppers like me and I knew that, if they tried to open the truck, the bomb would go off. I ran back and warned them off. It took a sweaty few minutes to convince them but a look in through the rear window at the piles of fertiliser sacks eventually convinced them and we got away just in time. In the havoc of collapsing buildings and the glass raining down from the towering office block at the end of the street, I slipped away back to my contact's flat in Kilburn. They're an unforgiving lot, the IRA; I was kneecapped for my mistake. If they knew I'd warned the panda crew, it would have been worse.'

'What do you mean "Kneecapped"?' Someone asked.

'It's an IRA punishment they put a gun to the back of your knee and blow your joint apart. You don't walk away from that I can tell you.'

'You haven't got a limp, though, have you?' David sounded suspicious of the story.

'Strangely enough, only about one in five victims end up with a permanent limp. I was one of the lucky ones. Lucky also, that they had the decency to throw me from a speeding car outside the A&E department of the West Middlesex Hospital. It was a long and painful recovery though. That was the end of my police career of course; invalided out with a Chief Inspector's pension. It also curtailed my dancing aspirations. So you can see my dear Diana I have good reason to be suspicious of Irish partisans. But I over reacted, for that I'm sorry.'

Chapter 6

It was afternoon on their first day in the raft and a sense of gloom had descended on the survivors. Despite the heroic tale of daring-do the policeman had regaled them with, few liked him and, although many disbelieved his account, none felt inclined to challenge him on it. The silence dragged on. It was Diana's turn to take a two hour stretch on lookout but she, for once, looked sound asleep.

Jenni looked at her watch and said softly, 'Diana. Diana, your turn outside.'
'Oh, let her sleep,' Ken said, 'I'll do her shift; the sun will be murder on her delicate skin.' Without waiting for a response he eased himself out of the hatch, 'I need a pee anyway,' he said.

Moments later, Adam, his face red and raw from staring into the sun, clambered inside. Jenni handed him a ration of water and watched him gulp it down gratefully. She gave it an hour, leaving her charges to their thoughts, before deciding they needed something more to pass the time.

The Orator's Tale

The older man with the boyish face and thinning, grey hair stared at his questioner as if he hadn't heard.

'I said it's your turn next. Tell us about yourself,' Jenni said again.

'Look, I'm not really sure I want to join in with this. I, er, I'm . . .'

'Don't I know you?' asked the man who had introduced himself in a strong Yorkshire accent as Postlethwaite.

'I don't think so,' the man answered, 'but you've probably seen me around the ship.'

'I thought I recognised him, too,' said Diana. 'Come on, give us your life story; you've got nothing else to do, have you?'

'I guess not. OK, my name is Turney, Ted Turney. I'm a Londoner. Well, I still call myself that although I haven't lived there since my middle-twenties; I'm sixty-seven now. I'm marr . . . I'm widowed . . . recently. Still trying to get used to the idea of not having a partner and being around people again.'

Passengers who hadn't wanted to play and were trying to ignore the game of introductions, looked up, turning their faces towards him. His voice was impossible to disregard. It was as warm and comforting as home-made apple pie but as commanding as a colonel's.

'Why not use this as a way of starting to talk again, Ted. It'll probably help,' Jenni coaxed.

Ted chuckled to himself as he spoke. 'Yes. Thank you, you're right. That's exactly the sort of advice I would have given. Hmnn, OK. Where to start?

'Let's see. I was what we call nowadays a baby-boomer, born after my father came home from the war to find our house and the one opposite the only ones standing for about ten streets around, apparently.

'It's incredible to think how young they were; my mum was a nineteen-year old nurse, dad was a war veteran at just twenty-one. All that death and destruction for . . . Anyway, my father became a policeman; perhaps he'd got used to wearing a uniform. He didn't advance in the force. He remained a beat-bobby as we used to call them; your friendly local policeman. Those were the days when there was respect for the man on the beat; he was the neighbourhood protector. It was a time of petty crime and too much to drink on a Saturday night, not drugs, rape and gang killings, like now. What a world, eh.'

He glanced around the passengers before resuming.

'The only gangs we knew were those in our street and the ones around us. I can see some of you are of an age to remember those "good old" days. We were the Black-hand gang; I was the leader, and our enemies on the bombsites were the Wolves. Boys only, of course, back then.'

Ted began to relax as he continued; after all, speaking for a living was how he'd spent most of his life. Without thinking, he threw in a witticism.

'Ah, those were the days, but you know what they say about nostalgia?' He paused. 'It's a thing of the past.'

A few people smiled at the old joke.

'So when did you leave London then, Ted?' Tony asked.

'Oh . . . Years ago, I'll get to that.' He smiled and went on. 'Somehow, I did well in education, ultimately getting into grammar school. My mum and dad were so proud, I remember, especially after a few years when I received my shiny Head Boy badge.' The memory brought a smile to his face. 'I was lucky enough to get a place at University so it would have been around the mid-sixties when I left London behind for the first time.

'Two years later I was back, having dropped out of uni and itching to earn money. Mum and Dad were disappointed but soon after had other things on their minds to worry about. Bizarrely, they were both diagnosed with cancer at the same time; prostate for my dad, colon for my mother. Nothing could be done, we were told.' Ted paused as he ran his fingers across the top of his head in thought. 'They were quite religious so, right up to the end, they believed, as they'd been good people all their lives, God would step in and save them. He didn't. Six months later, disillusioned, they died within days of each other. It's awful to lose a parent, as some of you will know, but to lose both at once is heartbreaking.

'Jump forward a few years to my mid-twenties; I was married with a pregnant wife and was doing well at work. After my parents' deaths, I got a job as a sales rep and worked my way up to area sales manager. We couldn't afford a larger house in London so I left the big city behind for the second and final time to move to Reading in Berkshire, which was convenient for my patch. I became a sales director but for various personal reasons left all that behind a number of years later to do something else. That's it, really. Who's next?'

'Come on, Ted, that's only half your life story,' the Yorkshireman complained. 'Where else have you lived and worked? I'm certain I've seen you before.'

'Well, I don't think we've actually met; I've got quite a good memory for faces. But it's possible you've seen me. I used to be . . .

'I'd better explain that. Let me go back to when I was a sales director. When I was working, one of the things I was recognised for was my ability to enthuse and motivate my sales teams at meetings. I suppose I had a good way with words and I'd always enjoyed the psychological aspect of persuasion. That's why I liked selling, I suppose. Public speaking is only selling, really; getting your audience to believe in what you're saying. Fast-forward a few more years. One day I was in a hotel giving such a talk to a group of managers; not mine, a colleague's. He'd, er, asked me to help him out as I was, let's say, in between jobs for various reasons.

'After it was over, I was approached by a man of about sixty who'd been listening at the door.

"I heard you mention God as I was passing the door," he said, an Irish lilt to his voice, "so I stopped to listen. I hope you don't mind."

'I told him it was no problem then asked him if he'd enjoyed it. I've always remembered his words; they brought back some of the confidence I'd lost since . . . Um, since . . . nothing.'

Like the experienced orator he was, Ted had been studying his audience. He believed he'd got away with his near slip.

'Anyway, he said to me, "Your talk was the most inspiring thing I have ever heard; it made me want to get back to my work and do better."

'I got a shock when he told me his line of work. He was a priest. He wasn't wearing a dog collar, simply old cords and a sweater. He looked more like a farmer than a clergyman. It turned out he was in the hotel helping to run a Christian conference, where they'd agreed to wear casual clothes. He told me they were worried that the sight of fifty or so collars would put the fear of God into other guests. We both laughed at his joke. He said he soon realised I hadn't been talking about God in my presentation but became fascinated by my message.

'He seemed a nice guy so I was happy to chat to him over a cup of coffee. I was kind of pleased he didn't ask about my beliefs. What happened next set me off on a new career. He asked if I'd give my talk to his meeting, although he couldn't pay me. I had nothing else on my agenda so I agreed to do it at the end of the afternoon as their closing speech. I did it; it went well and he was delighted.'

Turning his head, Ted met everyone's eyes, pleased to see their fascination with his story. This was the first time since his retirement, two years earlier, that he had spoken at any length to a group of people. He was beginning to enjoy the return of his feeling of pleasure at entertaining an audience.

'I forgot about it until a couple of weeks later when he phoned to ask me to do the same again at a different meeting. Paddy the Priest, he called himself. I don't know why I agreed as he couldn't pay me but, for whatever reason, I said yes.

'"We'll all be wearing our uniform,' he laughed. "Won't put you off, will it?"

"As long as you don't all try at once to convert me," I told him. "Will there be any miracles with all you holy people around?" I teased him.

'"You know what we say in Ireland about that subject, don't you, Ted?" he asked, "There's more miracles performed in a vat of Irish whiskey than in a whole church full of saints."

'So, I did it for him as he was such a lovely man. Afterwards, I watched as one of the younger ones made a beeline for me. Here comes the God speech, I thought. But I was wrong. He wanted to know if I'd ever considered putting my thoughts in print: writing a book. He asked if I would like an introduction to his brother who was a publisher. I thought, why not?

'The next week I met up with the man at his office near Russell Square in London. To cut a long story short, six months later my first book was published. We called it, "God Can't Do It On His Own". It was an incredible success; thousands sold in the first month and it was soon up for a reprint. On the back of that, I began touring the country giving speeches on my philosophies. And all thanks to Paddy. To capitalise on the success I wrote two more books over the following two years: "Will God Get You Going?" and "Can God Pay Out?" Thirty years later and, amazingly, they're all still in print. Although I've written more since, those are still the most popular. I wrote them all under the pen-name of Luke Godson.'

'I thought I recognised you,' said Tony.

'You're on the telly, aren't you,' said Postlethwaite, 'but you look different.'

'I used to wear a hairpiece and different glasses; the producers told me I had to look like I did when I wrote the books. Of course, that was ridiculous; I was in my thirties then. Last time I was on TV a couple of

Raft of Life

years ago, I was sixty-five. But they were paying me so what do you do?'

'Ted, what did you mean when you said about not wanting Paddy the Priest to convert you?' asked Tony.

'Oh, that. I didn't want to upset Paddy as he was such a great guy. You see I was, and still am, an atheist.'

The young lady with long legs who had introduced herself as Diana, one of the ship's entertainment crew exclaimed, 'An atheist! All that stuff you wrote and you say you're an atheist?'

'Yes, that's what I said; I'm an atheist,' replied Ted. 'I have never believed in God and never really understood the illogical thinking of those who do. I have more in common with Richard Dawkins, arch-unbeliever, than the Archbishop of Canterbury. Actually, both are quite nice people,' he smiled at his questioner, 'I've met them on TV and socially. Get them to park their hobby-horses somewhere and chat about other everyday matters over a drink and they're fine.'

Diana was almost frothing at the mouth as she went on the attack. 'But you write about God! What a bloody hypocrite!'

Ted spoke calmly, 'You say I'm a hypocrite. If I remember correctly, the dictionary definition is: a person who puts on a false appearance of virtue or religion isn't it? Have you read any of my books?'

'Three of them,' she said.

'Well, well. Thank you, Diana. And what did they do for you?'

'I'd been having a bad time. I suppose they helped me believe in myself again.'

'Believe in yourself. Good. And you believe in God?'

When she nodded, silently, Ted continued. 'Did you believe in God any more or less after you read them?'

'No, I don't suppose I did. Look Luke or Ted or whatever you call yourself now, don't try and get all silver-tongued with me!'

'Sorry. Silver-tongued am I?' Ted wanted to smile at that rather old-fashioned term coming from such a young mouth but restrained himself. 'OK, you make your point first and I'll just listen.'

With much finger-wagging and pointing, Diana put her point of view. A few other passengers sitting nearby nodded their agreement with the forthright woman.

'OK, got it,' said Ted. 'You're saying that because I use the word God in my book titles and referred to God in my writing and when I was on TV, people saw me as an evangelist preaching the word. Right, Diana?' He paused. 'Wrong!

'Take my first book, "God Can't Do It On His Own". Because the word is there, it doesn't make me a believer. When Harper Lee wrote To Kill a Mockingbird, she was neither a murderer nor bird-hater to my knowledge. And when her friend Truman Capote wrote about the true-life killers in his In Cold Blood, it didn't mean he admired those savages. Read the books again, if we ever get out of here that is, and you'll find nowhere do I say I believe in God nor do I exhort the reader to do so.'

'But . . .' Diana interrupted.

Ted talked gently over the interjection. 'What I say to the reader is, if you believe in a God – and I don't specify – then get him on your side to achieve the things that caused you to buy the book in the first place. I also urge people to get anyone else who is important to them on their side: parents, spouse, siblings, whoever; because their support helps to lighten the burden of starting to believe in yourself. But what I preach is, don't rely on any of them, including God, to do it for you. That's the only enlightenment I attempt to bring to people's lives.'

'But what about your name? I mean, Luke Godson, for goodness sake. If that isn't trading on God's name, what is?'

'Can I ask you, do you like Stefani Germanotta? Or is Marshal Bruce Mathers III more to your liking?'

'What are you talking about? I've never heard of them.'

'Marketing is what I'm talking about. Constantine the Great called the first Christian Ecumenical Council in Nicaea in 325 AD near Byzantium, or Constantinople as it became known in his honour, in order to straighten out a few little problems of belief between the churches so they could begin marketing Christianity. About seven hundred years later, they fell out and created two different Christian churches that had to market their ideas of God separately in competition with each other. Five hundred years on and King Henry VIII had another revolutionary idea. More marketing needed in Britain. Three hundred or so years after Constantine someone living across the sea rebranded it and marketed God and his prophet under different names. Strong marketing by both spread the 'good word' worldwide. In America in the nineteenth century, someone else rebranded it, changed the name and off we went again. And so it has continued; marketing using the name God. I didn't start it.'

'Sounds like one of my school lessons,' said Franny.

Julia joined in, 'Yes, come on, gives us a break!'

Joining in the discussion from out on watch, Ken Watts disembodied voice carried to them all, 'I find what Ted says very interesting. More people have died in wars, persecution, torture and murder carried out in God's name, often on a medieval Pope's instructions, than for any other reason. Did you know that? Look at the Crusades or the Inquisition or 9/11, for instance. I think publishing a few books hardly compares, do you?'

Ted acknowledged his support again then, leaning forward to make eye contact, continued addressing Diana, 'Those two people, by the way, are Lady Gaga and Eminem. Catchy names, aren't they? If they traded under their true names, they wouldn't stand a chance, no matter how talented.

'I've spent half of my life trying to motivate people towards self-belief so they can improve themselves. As you've read my books, you will know there are sections addressed to the unemployed as well as the CEOs of the world; to those with problem marriages; to secretaries and bosses; straight, gay; professors and students; and people from every walk of life.'

Someone sitting several seats away muttered, 'Too expensive for people on the dole.'

'Oh, I notice someone scoffs about books for the out-of-work. How could they afford the £14.99? I've never made a big thing about it but to answer your scorn, I'll tell you now that, over the years, I've distributed more than a hundred-thousand free books throughout the UK for the use of the unemployed. No, not because I'm a philanthropist; I'm not, but because I know that, the more people I can help to help themselves achieve things with their life the better the world will be. And, yes, before you say it, I've become wealthy in the process. But that doesn't make me a believer in Mammon either, no more than your salary does for you.'

***

Tony wanted to prompt more of the easy dialogue from the accomplished orator. For that reason, rather than out of interest in the man's one weakness, he asked, 'What was that you were saying the other night about having a problem with brandy?'

'Now that does sound like it might be an interesting story. Come on, spill the beans, Ted,' said Postlethwaite.

'We-e-ell, not sure about that. It's something I don't discuss, even with friends. In fact the only person who knows . . . damn, can't get out of that habit. The only person who knew was my wife, Anna. Oh, what the hell. Why not, we'll probably never see each other again and I don't have an *image* to worry about any more. When I was in my mid-thirties, I knew I was becoming an alcoholic.

'How did it start? My two lovely children had died several months before. No, I'm not blaming that, don't worry. I only blame my weakness. I was no more or less distraught than the millions of others who lose loved ones. I coped as well as anyone does. I was depressed but I felt I was handling it. I was trying hard to keep up to scratch at work. Then I discovered a new friend. Her name was brandy; any-brand brandy.

'A friend had recommended a "little drop of brandy in your breakfast coffee, it'll cheer you up." One morning on my travels, after waking in a tangle of hotel sheets, I took his advice. He was right. Eventually, I did the same with mid-morning coffee, sneaking it from a hip-flask I took to work. Then, after a while, I stopped bothering with the coffee altogether. My boss was as understanding as anyone could want, but a year after my kids died he fired me. I had become so unreliable; even I would have fired me.'

Ted shuffled in his seat as if uncertain whether or not to continue. He took a deep breath.

'I used to have a terrible dream. I still remember it as clearly as if it was yesterday. It was always the same.

'My knuckles scraped as I climbed the metal rungs inside a subterranean pipe. Above me, it was night-black; below me, even darker. Hand over hand, step after step I clung tightly, terrified of falling but more fearful of what awaited above. I was naked, shivering as if with a fever. My body felt worn out. After what seemed like hours but was probably a minute or two, my eyes cleared the surface. All around a war seemed to be raging. Men and women were kicking, gouging, beating each other; the air was rent with deafening screams. A body fell in front of me, its head at my level, death-eyes staring at me. I exited the pipe.

'In the centre of this mayhem a solitary male figure stood, illuminated from above by a blinding spotlight. It was a black man, dressed in a floor length black leather coat, similar to that guy in Matrix. He stood in a sea of vomit. In his hand was a bottle of brandy. I took aim with a pistol I seemed to have acquired; you know how you do in dreams. I held the gun with both hands and squeezed the trigger gently. I watched the bullet leave the end of the barrel, travelling in slow motion towards its target – the bottle. Instead of shattering it, the missile left a round 9mm hole just above the bottom. Amber fluid gushed out, glistening and golden in the light.

'The man laughed, tossing aside the empty bottle. The world had gone silent apart from his mocking laugh. He ran towards me, crouching. He removed bottle after bottle of brandy from within the voluminous coat, placing them on the ground with every step. As he neared me, I retreated and fell into the pipe, dropping feet first into the damp, deep, darkening nothingness. I landed as gently as a falling scrap of paper, at once fast asleep. Until the dream returned.'

'Oh my God, that's gross,' said Franny.

'Don't mention God,' Ken joked in an effort to lighten the mood.

'Is that when you gave up?' asked Helena.

'Unfortunately, no. An old friend had a villa in Spain and offered it to me for as long as I liked. "Till you get back into shape," he said.

'It was a bad idea, seen with hindsight, 'Ted rubbed his chin. 'I became well-known in the local bars. The nearest I got to food was a pint of beer and a bag of crisps. Over the following months, I was refused a drink in every establishment in the area and often taken home by my drinking cronies. After one such night, I awoke with the sunrise, lying on a garden lounger. As I got up, I tripped and fell into the swimming pool. Because of my inebriation, I was disorientated; floundering around, gulping water, not knowing top from bottom. I bumped into the steps and hauled myself half above the surface, coughing out pool water, belching up brown liquid vomit.'

'That's disgusting,' Clarissa said with repugnance.

Ted carried on with his tale. 'I came round many hours later, tried standing but passed out. This happened a number of times after darkness returned and I finally woke with the next dawn, my face lying in a swamp of regurgitated beer and brandy.'

'Enough, enough, please,' said Isobel.

'Oh, yuk! Too much information!' complained Julia.

Tony joined in. 'Come on, Ted, leave it out!'

'My legs were below water, half-kneeling on the steps. This time I rose, staggered indoors, drank several litres of water followed by coffee after coffee, black with sugar – but no brandy. I realised it must be over thirty hours since the boys dropped me off. Not only that, it was more than twenty-four hours since my body had been topped-up with alcohol and, for the first time in over a year, I believed it was the last thing it needed.

'I had breakfast, with tea instead of coffee, and contemplated my situation and reached a decision about my future. I needed to get back to the UK to try and make a fresh start.'

'Wasn't your wife there to help you?' Helena wanted to know.

'That's another story. I was married to someone else then, not my . . . ,' he struggled with the words, 'my late wife.

'In one of my books I address the subject. What I say to people with that problem is this: Think of it like a play. If you've just given up and are struggling then you've just exited the Stage but not the Theatre of Alcoholism. Heavy drinkers are like actors, waiting in the wings for their next line. Temptation is centre stage, ready to give the cue. You may never leave the theatre but you don't have to go back on stage. I recommend they try to remember that.'

'Don't you drink at all now, Ted?' asked Tony.

'I have an occasional glass of wine.'

'Have you ever been tempted "back on the stage" as you say?' asked Helena.

'It's often the loss of something valuable that creates the breeding ground for serious drinking. It might be a loved one, self-esteem, property or any number of things. My wife; as I said, not the one who was around in my drinking days, died six months ago which, in a way, is why I'm here.'

'Oh, I'm so sorry.' Helena looked embarrassed at her question.

'Thank you. Anna died from cancer – don't get me going on that subject. Unlike my parents, she didn't ask for nor expect help from any God. But she did expect something from the medical profession after the billions of dollars poured into research each year. Anyway, that was my hardest test, but with the support of the friends who encouraged me to come on this cruise, I've been doing alright.'

'Excuse me,' Julia clambered awkwardly onto her knees and crawled towards the open hatch, 'just need to powder my nose. Ken you keep your eyes on the horizon till I tell you.' She climbed outside knowing it wasn't a moment too soon.

'Ted . . . You said all this came about due to the loss of your children,' said Jenni, 'I can sympathise with that; it happened recently to, er, someone, to a friend of mine. Do you want to tell us about it?'

'As I've already been laying myself bare, I suppose I may as well carry on. Back in the late seventies when my kids were young, we all; that is, their mum, the kids and I, lived on the outskirts of Reading in Berkshire, as I mentioned. Although I was a Londoner, I couldn't afford to live there so, like many others, we moved out. Berkshire was convenient for my job.

'We had a small, detached house in a street of forty or so identical little boxes, advertised as suitable for 'up-and-coming' future executives. You know the sort of place. One new company car and one second-hand run-around for the wife. One parked in the drive, the other on the street. The guys got the hover mowers out on Sundays, occasionally followed by a beer at the local. The families were all similar: in their twenties or thirties with young children. My two, Georgie and Jamie, loved it there; they had plenty of friends to play with. Georgie was so pretty; everyone loved her short,

79

bubbly red hair that matched her vivacious personality. Jamie was blond and a typical rough-and-tumble boy.' Ted paused as Julia made her flustered way back to her seat.

'Sorry Ted, do go on.' She wrapped her arms around her knees and looked intently at the man, her interest peaked.

'My wife at the time loved living there too,' he went on, 'she'd had most of the men on the estate in the first couple of years, continuing a pattern of pretty much the whole of our married life. Except for the first year or so, that is, when we thought we were still in love. That's when the kids came along. I can't complain because I'd become just as bad. We had what I called retaliatory affairs. Actually, the word affairs has connotations of l'amour, doesn't it, but this wasn't about romance, it was simply revenge and sex. She'd go off with someone so I'd get even by doing the same which made her hit back at me by finding another man, and so it went. A sad and destructive relationship with only one thing in common, our children.'

Clarissa gasped; Jenni tutted.

'Yes, you're right to tut; it was a terrible situation and, to be honest, I can't believe I'm telling you about all of this. One thing in her favour, she tried to be discreet, and mostly succeeded in that, so the kids weren't aware, nor made the butt of any jokes at school. But as much as anything, it was reflective of the times in which we lived. We had grown up in the era of flower-power and free sex; girls had been going on The Pill in increasing numbers since the sixties.

Sleeping around was quite normal and just because one got married didn't mean it had to stop your fun.'

Postlethwaite interrupted, 'I once read a quote by Somerset Maugham: "A man marries to have a home, but also because he doesn't want to be bothered with sex and all that sort of thing."'

Ted joined in the laughter that seemed to be greater among the women than men. He was pleased someone had lightened the mood because what he was about to say would soon darken it.

He continued, 'Our street ran off the main road into town. Being an L-shape, it linked from there to another main route. Whilst it was generally a quiet area, during peak traffic times it was used as a short cut from one road to the other, avoiding the traffic lights at the nearby junction. Ours was a narrow street with cars lining each side so vehicles passing through usually drove slowly. It was the sort of diversion I would often use myself when out driving from A to B; we've all done it, haven't we?'

Several people nodded.

'As I said, Georgie and Jamie had plenty of friends where we lived. During off-peak times, it was quite safe for them all to play in the road or on each other's front lawns. They knew about the dangers between seven-thirty and eight-thirty in the morning and five and six in the afternoon. Generally that wasn't a problem as they were either getting ready for school or having their tea.'

Ted paused to swallow hard. He rubbed his temples as if easing a headache. The story he was to relate to the group of strangers was about one of the worst things that had happened to him. He could feel a burning behind his eyes as he swallowed again, then took a deep breath before picking up the threads of the tale he'd begun.

'One day, a sunny Friday in June, the thirteenth believe it or not, I'd managed to finish work early enough to collect the kids from school at three-thirty. Georgie was seven; Jamie, eight. They were inseparable; the pair of them played together, stuck up for each other, went everywhere hand-in-hand and loved one another like twins.' Ted hesitated before going on. 'We were home before four o'clock so there was still play time before tea and, on such a beautiful day, it would have been unfair to refuse them. I stood in the drive behind the car to watch them cross the road to their friends' house. The road was clear; they held hands as they stepped from the kerb.

'From the side of the house, three along to my right where the corner of the L was, came a roaring and screeching as a car skidded broadside into our part of the road. This was no ordinary short-cutting driver; the car was moving like a stunt car from a movie. The back end was twitching as it rocketed towards me; towards my children. It side-swiped a neighbour's car which did nothing to slow it down.

'People say you see these things in slow motion. If it hasn't happened to you, you will never believe just how slow. You will never realise how long two seconds can last; it is as if it began at the time you were born and is now ending. By the time I shouted, "Kids, come back!" it was happening. They were half-way across the road, Jamie holding on tight to Georgie's hand, when the car hit them at about forty miles an hour it was reckoned. They sailed into the air like a pair of nine-pins, somersaulting as the car shot below them without slowing. I saw Jamie's mouth moving but heard no sound above the thunder of the engine at full revs. Georgie's eyes were closed beneath a deep frown, as if wondering what was happening to her. At one point, with their arms outstretched, they reminded me of a Japanese painting; you know the ones of the cranes gliding past the mountain. As they fell towards earth, they struck the boot before bouncing onto the tarmac to rest on their backs. Then the killer was gone, tyres spitting loose gravel over their little bodies.'

Ted's voice was cracking as he struggled to control himself. 'I cradled them in my arms, kissing them, talking to them, willing them to say, "We're alright, Daddy" but, of course, that didn't happen. They were silent. They were motionless. They were dead. And they were still holding hands.'

Several passengers wiped their eyes and blew their noses. Julia, sitting next to him, put a comforting hand on Ted's shoulder.

After a few moments, Ted told the rapt listeners, 'They found the car about a mile away; it had been used in a hold-up at the petrol station on the corner of the main road. The driver was never discovered. That was twenty-odd years ago. Georgie and Jamie were buried in Reading; I visit when I can. So much for your God,' he said to Diana, 'not the only time he let me down, as you can gather.'

The dancer looked into her lap to avoid his stare. The remaining passengers were as silent as funeral-goers.

'Enough from me, I think,' said Ted, 'so who's got some happier stories?'

Chapter 7

The sad story of the Orator's life had left the mood on the raft gloomy to the point of depression. Jenni tried to break the mood with an issue of food and drink. With the sun going down Diana volunteered to take the watch she'd missed earlier. Ken, feeling protective, moved to sit half in - half out of the opening to keep an eye on her. They were facing another night with no sign of rescue. Jenni was determined to raise the mood before the light failed and they were left to their dreams, or would they be nightmares?

The Vicar's Tale

'Now here is someone who must have a tale to tell,' Jenni laughed. She could not help it because as Reverend Goodfellow, returning from a call of nature, lifted his cassock to clamber over her reclining body she got a clear glimpse of silk stockings and suspenders cladding his remarkably shapely legs. 'You seem to have been taken unawares by the emergency Alistair?' she grinned.

Realising his secret had been uncovered he decided to come clean. 'Yes, well, when the accident happened I was sitting in the main restaurant waiting for someone to join me. There were always people looking for a likely partner to share their evening. I guessed it would not be too long before someone, hopefully, interesting would make come along. As usual I had dressed, with meticulous care. I was now prepared for an enjoyable and different evening's entertainment.

I didn't have to wait long as a rather large and flustered man exploded onto a chair at my table and immediately began to tell me that the boat was going down and I should hurry to the life boats. He even offered to escort me and also keep me company. However, the Rev. Goodfellow could not be discovered as he then was. I jumped up from my seat and hurried to my cabin, on the pretext of picking up my life jacket. He made to follow me but I was successful in dodging my informant. What I really needed to get was my cassock and cloak to cover my evening finery and a pair of shoes more suitable to manage the stairways and ladders I knew I would encounter on my way to safety. All this diversion and necessary preparation made me somewhat tardy in reaching the lifeboats. There were now no more available, but I was saw this life raft being launched and putting all my faith in The Lord and Messrs Canepa & Campi,' he pointed at the manufacturers logo emblazoned on the canopy behind him, 'and followed it into the sea.' So here I am and it certainly appears to have turned into a very different night, didn't it?' He smiled and leaned back against the yielding side of the raft, closing his eyes.

'Is that it?' Jenni, laughed. 'OK vicar I'll let you get away with that.'

Come now vicar perhaps you'd like to tell us your story. ' Julia encouraged him, 'you must be used to talking to people like your congregation, and all.'

'I'd rather not,' Alistair replied, 'well not yet, but I am a good listener too.'

'Hang on,' Ken sensed there was more to Alistair's story, 'come on, tell us why you came on this cruise all alone in the first place . . . or maybe you do have a secret companion?'

'I really don't know why you should say that. My dear wife, Margaret, is gone, a huge blow to me. She was not just my wife, but my ever helpful companion and also my best friend. She assisted me with all matters in the parish and my Bishop was constantly reminding me how lucky I was, as if I didn't realise that already. However even my beloved Margaret didn't know my secret.'

'Sounds very intriguing.' DJ leaned forward across the jumble of legs that filled the centre of the raft to look into Alistair's face. 'What deep, dark happenings have you been hiding? Has it anything to do with the lady seen leaving your cabin of an evening?'

'Yes,' said Ken, a cruel glint in his eye. 'We never see her around during the day, but she's always at dinner dressed to the nines – not quite your taste vicar, I would have guessed.'

'More to my taste than you can ever imagine.' Alistair reddened.

'Come on Guys,' Jenni intervened, 'give him a break.'

'No - no,' Ken was adamant, 'we're all bearing our souls here, it's the least we can expect from a man of the cloth.'

'Oh well, under these circumstances, I suppose I should come clean and confess all.' Alistair adjusted the cassock he had suffered throughout the heat of the day for fear of revealing what lay beneath. Now the air was cooling he once more put off the embarrassment knowing that now it had dried out he would need it as night attire. 'I've said it myself plenty of times to others, confession is good for the soul, I should now take my own advice.'

'Back in those days I worked tirelessly and conscientiously all week and always gave of myself wholeheartedly to my parishioners, often above the call of duty. But, Wednesday evenings were mine to do exactly what I wanted to do. Margaret went to her quilting circle, in the village, so this meant I had three or four hours all to myself. Well that's not quite true because then I used to live it up with the boys.

'I never drank alcohol at home, so at a village pub, quite remote from my own, I used to enjoy an evening free from restraint, an evening of wine, a woman and song – well darts or cards with the boys as I said before.'

'Do you still indulge yourself when you are home?' Ken, still oblivious to what Jenni had seen asked. 'Who was the woman? The mysterious lady of your evenings on the cruise?'

'The answer to your first question is emphatically no and this is the reason why. One evening, returning home from a most enjoyable Wednesday night out, I found the Bishop parked in my drive on a very much unexpected visit. He caught Alison just as she let herself in to the house.

'Alison! The mysterious lady friend – really vicar?'

'Now I must explain further. At the beginning of each Wednesday evening, Alison was reborn from a locked suitcase kept in my study. A suitcase that contained all that made up Alison. The finest silk and lace underwear in a dazzling array of colours, several pairs of fishnet stockings, some high heeled shoes – very elegant but of rather a large shoe size, about half a dozen party dresses, all very flattering and dare I say quite sexy, assorted wigs and a selection of jewellery. There was also a smaller case, which was crammed with every conceivable item of ladies makeup. Then with practised aplomb, Alistair was transformed into the delectable Alison ready for an evening's enjoyable, but really quite innocent, fun. Of course, the Bishop demanded an explanation and I just collapsed under his interrogation. The shame and disgrace that followed my revelations were unbearable for both Margaret and me. She left, while I was in retreat. This had been suggested, no . . . demanded, by the Bishop. I was to receive counselling to sort out my perverse and in his words, unnatural behaviour.

'Of course it didn't work and Margaret was gone for good. Her Wednesday evenings were her secret – an affair with a local tradesman – huge scandal again.

'I left the village, under a cloud, never to return and decided on this cruise, but Alison refused to be left behind. She made her entrance for the evening while Rev. Goodfellow supposedly rested in his cabin. I think that answers all your queries and I quite understand if you now find my company unacceptable. I shall endeavour to keep myself to myself.'

'Bit difficult to do that, old man, in our present circumstances' DJ spoke gently. 'I think I speak for most here; we're all in the same boat now, sorry no pun intended, and you're definitely one of us, life raft crew. So welcome to you and Alison too! Trust we get to meet the lady properly, some day.'

Franny was fascinated and found it all amusing. By the time the Reverend Goodfellow had finished speaking, she was giggling uncontrollably. For a few moments, all her fears and concerns forgotten.

'That's a very pleasant sound,' remarked Ted.

She tilted her head enquiringly.

'Your laughter.'

Franny felt embarrassed. Her aunty was missing, she was among strangers and she was laughing. Would they think she didn't care; that she was only a kid, so couldn't possibly understand how serious this really was.

Chapter 8

Sunset was briefly spectacular but once it dipped below the horizon, the purple sky rapidly darkened. The moon was yet to rise and Diana couldn't help marvelling at the night sky. 'When you look up there,' she said to Ken, 'how could you ever deny that God has a hand in all this.' The firmament was ablaze with millions of stars, awe inspiring to even the most cynical of souls.

'I never denied God, just the organisations that exploit his splendour,' he said gently.

Everyone took a turn at coming out to admire the sight until a full moon rose to dim the stars with its searchlight brilliance. They settled down for the night, humbled but with a greater sense of isolation.

The survivors seemed to adjust their body clocks to daylight, so it was that, as the sun rose over the featureless horizon, they were almost universally awake. The air retained the cool of the night and a stiff breeze had sprung up. Many still retained their foil covers to keep out the draught.

The Cypriot's Tale

Helena sat so quietly in the raft that it was easy for everyone to think of themselves rather than her. But, although coping well with the awful conditions she felt the need to join in, make her point and share

91

experiences in case they failed to be rescued or make land at some time.

She coughed as loudly as her tiny body would allow and said, 'I am Helena Philipa Papas and I am from Cyprus. I have listened to you all with care and understand how different our lives are; we passengers and crew of the fated ship that we were on. I am alone here and have no idea what has happened to my beloved husband; Nicholas. We were separated as we queued No matter how I cried out; no-one listened or helped me to find him. As I searched and search I became lost myself. I cannot remember how I ended up in the sea but eventually I found myself being put into this craft.

Nicolas and I have been married for a lifetime and I am not sure I can go on without him much longer. I want to tell you about my life because it is so different to any of you.

I come from a small village and am old enough to remember times of hardship. We are in trouble now, here on this raft. I have known a life of real poverty in materialistic terms but one with a wealth of the spirit and so it may help some of you make a balance in your hearts for what you still enjoy because you are alive.

I shall have to travel with you to the time of my grandmother. She was born in the late eighteen seventies; about the time that Cyprus came under British Rule. She died in 1953 at the age of 70.

Every woman had to know all the jobs needed on the land to survive. She had to know how to tie the wheat and the barley; the main crops, into sheaves, how to follow closely the mower so as not to lose time. To help in bundling up the sheaves as these would be transported on mules or donkeys to the threshing field. The threshing started and would last all July and August according of course how big was the bundle of wheat or barley. A farmer grew both. The woman, seated on the wooden board, guided the animals such as oxen or mules to go round and round the threshing field for days, or weeks, until the ears released the wheat or the barley. Then, late in the afternoon, if there was no wind, they would make it into a heap. The winnowers, with special wooden shovels, would work for hours to separate the wheat or the barley from the straw. The wife was present helping.

After all this work, a substantial dinner followed with plenty of village wine. It is interesting to mention that the winnowers would not expect any money for this job. They helped for friendship, as a favour. The harvest took almost all the summer. The woman would follow the ploughman to sow or to pick the potatoes, to sow the seeds of the watermelon, of the kidney or haricot bean and go round in about a week to add seeds where they failed to sprout. When they started to produce fruit she had to store for the months that would follow as each crop came once a year. I doubt if there was any money for housekeeping. Even if there were, there was only one shop in the village, which sold wine and sometimes salted sardines and kippers. Of course, her most important issue was to preserve food that would keep them through the winter.'

Franny was intrigued by the old woman's calm and philosophical approach to life and moved to squeeze in alongside her to hear the faint and faltering voice better.

'The work on the land had absolute preference,' Helena continued. 'It was a matter of survival. There were no working hours. They worked from sunrise to sunset. The housewife had to prepare three meals a day for the people working on the land. For breakfast, she would make a soup, which they ate early in the morning at home. For lunch, she would prepare a pilau with pourgouri or she would boil potatoes for salad with any other vegetables they might have at the time. In this case, they would take along a bottle of olive oil with vinegar. They would all come home for dinner, which was usually pulses, boiled with some wild vegetables they might have found on the land. Perhaps I should mention that they did not find seed oils; they used olive oil if and when they had it. Instead, they melted the lard when they slaughtered the pig and, sometimes, the tail of the lamb. In the summer evenings, one neighbour would make some dough and invite the other neighbours to come and help in making noodles .She would provide, or even borrow, plenty of straw trays; the neighbours would come, sit around outside the house for a couple of hours and make the noodles. It is a pleasant occupation, it needs hardly any skill. The noodles would be dried and kept for winter. When she had enough, another neighbour would take over. I would like to mention that this cooperation gave me a feeling of security as a child of that period.

'Can you please stop talking about food, I'm starving.' Realising all eyes were on her, Franny burbled, 'It sounds a mainly vegetarian meal and a lot

94

of preparation.' She had sat as quiet and relatively unnoticed as the lady now telling her tale. She wasn't sure whether the people around her were being kind, not wanting to upset a young person seemingly on her own, or whether she was just unnoticeable to them. She was certainly not feeling her usual bubbly self. She was a strong willed young lady normally; happy to get into the thick of any fun or debate, but after all she had been through recently, she certainly wished she was invisible. All she desired was to be left in peace. She was cold, miserable and most of all scared. She didn't think she had ever felt so alone.

Franny had expected the old lady to be boring. She certainly seemed unlike anyone else she had ever met and she hadn't the faintest notion where the country they were talking about was; Cyprus did she say? Helena had continued to tell them about the life of the women in her grandmother and mother's era. Someone shouted out what hard work it must have been and Franny couldn't have agreed more. She found the tales fascinating and horrifying in equal measures and thought what a different life her family had known.

Coming back to the moment, Franny had realised Helena was talking about food again. Dishes she had never heard of and not the first notion what they might be but she was so hungry and her outburst came without a moment's pause for thought 'I-I'm sorry to interrupt your story is so interesting please go on' Franny blushed.

'It is quite alright, Pedhi-mou . . . I will tell you of other things, shall I?

'Please . . . did your mother get to do anything besides working in the field and cooking?' Suddenly aware the adults, still watching her intently, might think it rude of her to interrupt; she slumped back and huddled into herself. Helena rewarded her with a warm, gentle smile.

'The village woman was always looking for some chance to stay home around the house and devote time to her home. In those days, housekeeping had other priorities. The village woman had to be mistress of many crafts. She had to know how to make bread.'

'Food' said Franny, but this time with a smile.

'To do the special washing in a big basket which, although it sounds simple, needs some specialised knowledge. She had to be able to make thread using flax, cotton, or even cocoons. Quite often they would buy a whole fleece to make thread and weave the woollen sheets to use in winter.

She had to know weaving; it is not a simple craft. The village woman had to weave the material for her dresses, for her husband's shirts and even for his breeches. I remember this clearly as they used to send the material to Morphou to be dyed .They even had to weave the material for the household sheets, towels and tablecloths and the entire dowry. Quite a number of them used to sew their dresses as there were only two dressmakers in the village. Later more women learnt the craft.

When Helena paused, Franny said quietly, 'Excuse me, Mrs Papas, were you born in the village?' I mean, it sounds so hard a life for everyone. What if they got sick? Did they even have hospitals in Cyprus back then?' This time she sat back, pleased that she had asked, as peeking under her lashes, Franny noticed all the adults were listening as intently as she was to a description of the medical care and she thought of her recent visit to a Miami hospital.

If I am correct, until the middle thirties there were not even midwives in the village. When there was a need, a relation would bring one from a neighbouring village. She came riding on the donkey while the relative walked along.

Round the early thirties a typhoid epidemic spread in the village. Many people died as in those days they did not have suitable medicines.

Recreation was limited within the village. Everybody took part in the weddings which lasted a week. Both the young boys and the young girls were there, waiting for their chance to start dancing. The boys; two at a time, would start dancing showing their bravery; they often stopped to sing and express their feelings. When the girls had their chance, they would dance two at a time, showing their modesty, their dignity, looking always down.

At Christmas and Easter they organised musical gatherings. Quite often they went to the fairs usually on mules or donkeys .My grandparents would feed the animals, get them ready and throw a hand woven blanket on top, take a bottle of water and set off. My grandmother would take some pourgouri, flour, pulses and whatever she had in the house. In the years between 1930 and 1932 there was serious drought. My parents used to speak of poverty. They still had to pay the same heavy taxes as they paid during the Turkish rule. Soon the British cancelled the tax on the wheat.

Money was still scarce. The interest was high. In every village a usurer appeared. Many people lost their land for the simple reason of needing some wheat to feed the family. In our village there was some cooperation. I have been told of people helping their co villagers by giving them wheat to feed the family in return of work during the harvest of wheat and barley.

With the beginning of the Second World War, the village, like many more villages, started changing. The men, especially the ones without a lot of land, started going out for work. Many chances of work appeared. Money always brings change

Public communication was almost non-existent. There was the train that passed by our village and stopped in one of our fields.

In nineteen-forty-two my father, after a lot of consultations with friends, decided to send me to Nicosia to attend the Secondary School. I was the first girl to leave the village. Years after, I appreciated my father's brave decision and at the same time the support of my co-villagers. Life was difficult with the war so near in Greece and the Middle East. There was only one bus in the neighbouring village of Katocopia; the number was 40.This bus would take us to Nicosia to school and bring us back for Christmas.

The village started changing. Some progressive people bought the first harvesting machine and later a combined threshing machine. Both men and women were freed of the anguish of the harvesting and threshing that took up most of the summer.

In the early fifties, the first co-operative shop was opened in the village and the village woman had access to more kinds of food. At the same time, the shops were full with all sorts of useful items. The village woman could purchase what she needed for her household. She did not have to weave or sew her own garments. I must mention that, fortunately, some kept weaving as a hobby, mainly to weave the dowry stuff. The village now had its first midwife and soon, another two, and more dressmakers, came to make the life of the woman easier.

'So the village woman was free to take more initiative in planning and managing the land. New products appeared in the village. Carrots and beetroot and a more extensive cultivation of potatoes; all these were exported to England and more European countries. About the same time, people started planting citrus. There was a lot of optimism in our village and the neighbouring area. Some people would say that there were no poor in our village. There were poor but they lived well; as there was always work and enough food for everybody. The poor were free to pick food for their family from most fields, as long as it was for their personal use. In all this euphoria; with the trees full of fruit, the potato seed ready to be planted and the fields watered ready to plant, it was a crisis to accept the unacceptable; the invasion. We fled, we went anywhere we would find a roof over our head.' Helena closed he eyes and allowed the canvas behind her to take the weight of her head for a moment. Memories flooded her brain.

'I am rested now, my friends.' She opened her eyes, hooked her arm around Franny, who nestled into her bony side. 'I want to tell you more of my life. I know that, because it so different to all of you here, you may wish to hear more. I can tell that my storytelling has reminded many of you of how fortunate we all have been so far. It must rest with God, I think, if we survive to remember and retell our lives to others.

'My mother had a friend who used to come to our house and stand in the big door. When my mother asked her to come in, she hesitated and said, "Send your daughter out to play and I can come in and sit with you."'

Helena patted Franny's arm as she recalled the scene. 'I ran out to meet my friends. This picture stayed in my mind for years. Years later, my mother started to tell me the story of her friend who was called Yiota. She remembered that I was not very happy because I was made to go out while she visited. I must tell you about the misfortune, as it has made me be grateful for my life, husband and family even more.

'It seems that, in the years 1930 and 1932, there was a serious drought in Cyprus. The farmers of our village would get up in the morning, look up to the sky, and pray for some rain. It was in those years that an epidemic of typhoid fever broke out in the village and I lost my sister at the age of twelve. Soon after, some young men died of tuberculosis.

'Yiota was engaged to be married to Christos, a handsome, hard working young man. Her elder brother, Andreas, was already married to Maria, a rich girl with three brothers. Andreas was handsome and hardworking; he was happy to cultivate and farm the many pieces of land that his wife owned. Also Andreas was considered the best dancer in the village.

'Everybody blessed Maria and said how lucky she was to have married such a lovely man. After a couple of years, Andreas lost his desire to work. Every day he felt weaker, he spent more and more time in bed and soon he died. The village women felt sorry for the handsome young man, but sorrier for his wife who, at the same time, was expecting a baby.

'His parents and his sister Yiota were heartbroken. Maria gave birth to a lovely boy. Yiota realised how difficult it was for Maria to deal with the loss of her husband, manage the work on the land and bring up the baby.

She took a generous decision and said, "I shall ask Christos, my fiancé, to go every morning to Maria's house. He can take the oxen and cultivate all the land to get it ready for sowing."

'Everyday, Christos would get up very early in the morning, go to Maria's house, yoke the oxen and go to the different fields to cultivate and later, to sew the barley and a little later, the wheat. Soon he realised that the oxen were not well looked after, not well fed. When he told Maria, she confessed that she could not get up in the middle of the night to feed the oxen and have them ready for work early in the morning as she had to wake up many times to feed the baby.

'Soon Christos was sleeping on a plank in the straw room; near the stable and he got up at dawn and fed them. For a short time everybody was happy and so were the oxen as they were well fed. He felt at home. Maria would try and cook every day, as she was breast feeding and needed to eat a good dinner. When it started to become cold, she would burn pieces of wood outside in the open yard and then bring the charcoal in a tin container into the room. There was one room where she cooked, had supper and slept

'Christos worked hard in the fields, both summer and winter. He would go in to talk with Maria about the work and the plans of the following days or weeks. He stayed for coffee and soon he stayed for supper. He would share some potatoes; made tasty with cumin. Her brother, Giorgos, brought it to the house. So, day by day, Christos felt really at home. He would come in for a cup of coffee; he would pick up the baby to allow her to finish the food she was preparing.

'When it became very cold, Christos ended up in the big room sharing the double bed with Maria. All three of them lived in sheer bliss. In a village, big or small, nothing stays secret. Everybody is interested what goes on in the life of the neighbour. The women whispered in church until almost everybody knew and the story reached her brother.

'Giorgos was frantic. He went to Maria and started telling her off, threatening to kill both of them. He said that Christos must promise to marry her. It was a matter of honour, as the brothers were ashamed to walk in the kafenion. They would have to kill him to get rid of the shame.

'Maria planned a good supper and, while they were eating and having some wine she told Christos that her brother would kill him unless he was prepared to marry her. Christos was lost. He thought of his fiancé, Yiota, who was so kind and generous, of his parents and then of the whole village. He knew he had no alternative but to agree to marry Maria.

'The wedding took place one evening in the village church; the only people present were the three brothers and Christos' parents. Yiota was heartbroken.

She realised that she did not have a promising future. If an engagement was broken, it was almost impossible for the girl to get engaged to a suitable boy from the village. She developed tuberculosis, like her brother Andreas, but she lived for a number of years as a single, unfulfilled woman.

'This was the reason, the only reason, that I was sent out to play when she came visiting. I am sure you will agree that we may have many of our own difficulties but, compared to this life of hers, they may be nothing.' Helena looked around her as she finished the tale, hoping that its sorrow had made others feel less sorry for themselves.

DJ had been listening to Helena quite keenly, when Ken spoke out.

'So why are you so hell bent on telling us about Cyprus rather than yourself? he said. 'Don't you have a life?'

'Hey, hang on there you miserable old sod,' DJ's response was instant. 'You just keep your views to yourself. I bet you are the only person of any interest to you anyway. Most of us are finding this quite enlightening and can see the point of Helena's tales. Why don't you get a life as they say back home?'

He turned back to the frail old lady, 'Go on, Helena, tell this person the real reason for your approach to your life story and put a stop to his complaints. We've heard plenty from him, more than enough actually.' DJ relaxed in his place as others around him murmured their approval of his reply.

'Well, it has been my experience in life that history, and God come to that, predict how we will behave so as to benefit mankind with our existence. My past, the village life and family, taught me how to manage in times of difficulty, to appreciate what I have and who I am. I know that these conditions are nothing that any of us has gone through before. By telling you how our people lived during hard and unusual periods, I was hopeful that we could take comfort in remembering how lucky we have all been. I miss my Nicholas more than you can understand but I owe it to him and the family not to cry, just to survive and put my faith in God.' She sat and faced Ken as she spoke.

'Thanks Helena,' DJ added, 'we can all be so selfish. Yours is a good lesson in humility and, by Jove, some of us still need to get some. We need to save ourselves while we wait and see if there is a rosy future out of all of this. I only hope so, because I've a lot to do, and apologise for, when we get home, not forgetting the insurance claim as a first job.'

It had surprised Helena to discover that many of the other people on the raft hadn't even thought about Cyprus as a place, let alone know where it was.

'I must admit your stories are so different; how can you remember everything about your own life and so much of others?' Ken was contrite, 'I suppose it tells us that, to you, family has always been important. I feel guilty that it's just now that I think of my family and miss them. Last night I started to try and recall my own family members and could only manage a few.'

Helena had smiled gently when DJ had come forward and made his comment. It had shamed Ken into confessing to being a seemingly shallow person. 'Please don't apologise to me.' she said, 'I am not worldly like so many of you. My family is, and always has been, my world. Can I say more of my life?'

Several nodded so Helena continued her recollections.

'When I was a child, we had our holidays in the Marathasa valley on the northern slopes of our beautiful Troodos mountain range. The village we went to, I remember, was famous for its sulphur springs and became a regular place for us to go when the work in the fields had been finished for the season. By this time, at the end of July, the potato seeds; a piece of grown potato with an eye, had been planted carefully with my mother watching to ensure each new planting was good. Only then did my father tell my mother to start preparing to go to the same house that we used each year for our holiday.'

'I can't believe you went to the same place every year. Wasn't it boring?' Franny was taken with the old person's perspective on life.

'Not at all, it was what we were used to. We were fortunate. Many families could not afford even that in those days,' Helena smiled maternally at the youngest member of the company as she went on.

'So my mother would start getting ready. She packed all of our bed and table linen and, in between the layers, the crockery was packed to keep it from breaking. Food such as pourgouri, using the wheat crop, was made ready. Broad beans were cracked and packed along with other pulses. Olive oil, halloumi and olives themselves were taken. All that we took, and it was a lot, came from our own fields, prepared with our own hands so to say. If there were still watermelons we took them. As a last job my mother would make bread for us and those we left behind to tend the fields.

The mountain villages were chosen for summer time. My mother, and the other women, along with us children stayed there the whole summer. A husband only came at the weekends. We travelled on the bus, which my father arranged. It took many people, and time, to get everything on the bus. Before we went most of the village had come to wish us off. The driver and his assistant were fed with our fresh bread and food before driving us the long way to the mountains. My aunt arranged the blessing of the bus and its passengers with a small coal-fired burner, on which olive leaves were burnt. Prayers were said, we crossed ourselves and said our own private prayers. It took a time to say farewells and then the journey began.'

'I think we could have done with someone doing that before the Ocean Eco Star set sail, don't you?' someone interrupted. Several passengers laughed in agreement.

Helena smiled weakly before continuing her tale. 'I suffered from travel sickness, so was pleased to have stops. The village became very close to my heart and made the unpleasant travelling worthwhile. Of course, in the early days, there was no electricity. We loved watching the lady who had the job of climbing a wooden ladder to the paraffin lanterns, cleaning them, filling them with fuel and finally lighting each one along the streets. It was so different to home where, when the sun set, it was always dark outside.'

'It sounds so primitive, Helena,' Franny commented.

'Maybe, but it was all we knew. August was the busiest of the months for holidays in the mountains and buses arrived frequently. Home owners in the village became landladies in those times and I suppose it would now be called an early version of the tourist industry.

'The sulphur water used in the village was brought by donkey from the spring in metal containers. These were heated by the home owners for their guests and great use was made of the water, even for washing; after soakings as it was so soft to the skin.

'Rich Egyptians came, as did Cypriots who were living and working in Egypt. The villages in the Troodos area all became noisy and full of holiday guests. The days were spent walking, visiting the cafes and churches. One church remains in my memory because it was so special; it was called the church of Theoskepasti. A giant tree protects the church surroundings and it is forbidden to cut even a small branch; the Virgin Mary is said not to allow it to be altered, as the tree protects from enemies.'

Diana, the dancer, glared at Ted with a look that said, "don't you dare say anything about that." Ted recognised that stare; his wife used to do the same to him.

Helena carried on without noticing. 'We went to all of the other villages and in one, the first hotel was built. Many of us travelled together so that nothing was missed, people knew the way and experiences could be shared; such as seeing the sulphur springs up close. I can smell the strong, acrid smell by just putting my mind to those days. Wherever we were invited to go, we went. In those days many mountain people had their own orchards and vineyards. All these fields were small and on rising slopes of land; very awkward to work and crowded with plants. So, as a young person used to acres of land under cultivation, I was made to appreciate more of what we had. Cherish our fortunes anew.

'Evening time shows would be put on by professionals with their puppets. Both children and grownups laughed at the things that entertained them. But I know that my favourite was to visit the Cafe Paradisos with friends of my age. We talked about our own homes, books we had read and, as Cypriots do nowadays, we discussed world affairs, hoping to solve the country's problems. For us, the world stood still in the Cafe. There were some shops but life was simple so that we bought our food to cook and fruit to eat, supplementing things we bought with us. If my mother bought a chicken to cook she would kill it and truss it herself, being suspicious of one prepared by another woman.

'It was about 1955 I have not been to the holiday village since then. Things have changed as I understand and, of course, the young people today would not think of going there, let alone accompany their parents. It is often possible to see the old buses kept as an attraction now; cars being used in their place for all needs. I am a person of the old Cyprus, I know, but my memories are precious and many. Forgive me for going on so long, but then, time is meaningless in our situation.'

'Hear hear, Helena. Well spoken! I must say your sense of humility is a real eye-opener,' said Julia.

'It's a great shame no-one else in this motley crowd appears to have the same attitude. Anyway, God alone knows what - if any - future lies ahead for us after this nightmare. We can but hope. But if we do get out of here, you can be sure the top item on my to-do list will be to put in a hefty insurance claim. We should get millions.'

Raft of Life

Chapter 9

The swell had increased to a more noticeable roll and one or two had gratefully accepted the offer of sea sickness pills with the midday water ration.

The Soldier's Tale

Jenni looked across to where Adam slumped against the side of the hatch. 'What about you, Major Stone? You've been quiet up to now, surely you have a fascinating catalogue of army tales to tell.'

Stone, a little red faced, eased himself up to sit at attention, 'Yes, well, I have to either shut the world out or give in to panic, Jenni. It's just my way of dealing with my fear.' He looked sheepishly round the faces that had almost all turned towards him.

'Yes, fear is the right word. Among other things I'm terrified of drowning.'

'Aren't we all,' Tony murmured, 'especially now.'

'But that's only one of a long list of things I'm afraid of. Basically, I'm a coward.'

'But you were a Major in the army. Surely it took a lot of courage to achieve that rank,' said Ted.

'I'm . . . As it is confession time, I had better own up. To start with, I'm not a Major, unless you count being a major fraud. I assumed the rank when I went into banking. No one ever asked me to prove it and it does wonders for your credibility. That business is all about trust. Except, on reflection, it is not trust as

111

honest people like you know it; it's more about honour among thieves.

'As an officer and a gentleman, you can be trusted not to rock the boat,' he chuckled, 'present situation excluded,' He leaned back against the rafts canopy and nearly fell out through the unsecured flap. His fingers clutched at the rubber sides to regain his balance.

Ashen faced, he swallowed hard and forced a wan smile. 'Perhaps I should tell you about my illustrious military service.' He turned and zipped up the corner of the hatch behind him. 'In case I forget,' he grinned.

'Yes, I had a spell in the army. It wasn't optional, it was that or prison. I was only a kid, adolescent and wild. Fearless in those days I suppose. They found in me a talent for mechanical things and put me in the Royal Engineers. Never one for killing, it suited me too. I thought that a technical trade would keep me away from death.

'I saw enough in the Middle East, though, clearing up after IEDs. Bits of bodies among the wreckage, we had to recover what we could. Once, I found an eye under a chunk of truck bodywork; nothing else, just an eye. I lifted up a piece of metal and there it was looking at me. Blue it was, not even bloodshot, just staring back at me, the optic nerve strung out behind. I nearly threw up all over it. After that, all the other bits seemed ordinary. I realised that if I stayed, I would end up like all the others. Careless of the carnage, immune to the suffering of others, so I got out.

'That's what I told myself anyway. The truth is, I was afraid one day it would be my eye someone found waiting to be puked on. I went absent without leave.

'They caught me, of course, banged me up for a while then threw me out; dishonourable discharge. I'd made it all the way to Turkey. That's where I met my Jennifer. She was an aid worker in a refugee camp. She kind of adopted me when I staggered in from the desert; let me stay and help.

'At first it had been easy to get myself away from my base. I hitched lifts with other units, walked a bit, stole a bit, did some looting, you know, anything to survive. Then the MPs got the word out, so I lost the uniform and went native. There are some good people out there. Give you the thawb off their backs and share their last morsel of food. I drifted with them towards the border. The closer we got, the more officials we encountered; all corrupt. They robbed us blind . . . and worse.'

The raft rocked gently, wavelets rippled soporifically against its sides. He took a sip from his drink, looked around at the assembled company, wiped his lips on the back of his sleeve and went on.

'There was this one time when an army jeep came roaring up the road. I hid in the ditch, as usual, as soon as we saw its dust. They skittered to a stop alongside our party. peppering the group with flying stones.

'There were four militia, all with automatic weapons; Kalashnikovs. They started shouting; one fired a burst into the air. They were demanding to see papers and set about ripping the women's burkas away to show their faces. There were seven in our party not counting me. Hasim, who was about eighty but looked to be over a hundred, his son Ahmed, Ahmed's wife Anna and their four children, three girls and a boy. The soldiers started laughing. I peered over the lip of my hiding place to see them dragging Anna and her eldest daughter towards the jeep. One of the soldiers, a hook nosed, swarthy man in a dirty headdress and the uniform of the local guard, was training his gun on the others. I thought he was looking straight at me and froze to the spot.

'The other soldiers were forcing the women into the back of the jeep. The girl cried out with pain as one twisted her arm and the boy, eight-year-old little Hasim, ran to help. The guard shot him in the leg, sending him sprawling headlong in the dust and when his father ran forward, he felled the man with a vicious blow to the back of the head. Then they all climbed into the jeep and roared away towards the border. I was so ashamed I had done nothing to help.

'The remaining girls ran to their brother who was sobbing uncontrollably, not at his injury you understand but at what had happened to his mother and sister. Old Hasim picked his grandson up and hugged him close. Blood from the boy's leg left a vivid red stain on the old man's white thawb. Ahmed was coming round and, once he regained his senses, I helped him to dress the boy's wounds. The bullet had gone right through the lad's calf muscle. It must have been so painful but all I saw in the boys face was anger and defiance.

'There was nothing we could do except trudge on in the same direction the jeep had taken. We took it in turns to carry the boy. All the time I held him, I felt his little chest heaving but he no longer made a sound. I tried to apologise to Hasim for my inaction but he was quick to dismiss this saying, in our mix of his broken English and my few words of Arabic that if I had been found in their party, they all would have been shot. However, I knew that that was never my consideration. I was just too scared, plain and simple.

'Three hours later, we found Anna raped and beaten to death by the side of the road. A hundred yards further on, her daughter Maria. She was alive but bleeding from under her skirt. She was fourteen years old.' Tears formed in the corners of his eyes and he looked shamefaced down into his lap. 'So that's me, a cowardly Corporal.'

'But you made good, later didn't you,' Ted said, 'in civilian life.'

'I don't know about good . . . I made money, sure. For what good it did me.'

'You mentioned . . . Jennifer, was it?' asked Julia, 'I'm guessing you loved her.'

'You're a very attentive listener my dear,' he smiled, 'Jenny, yes I loved her; I guess I'll never stop, but that's another story.'

'Go on then,' Franny insisted, 'I love a good romance. Were you very young; and deeply in love?'

Adam was not sure whether she was being sarcastic or not, so he said, 'Do you really want to hear about her?'

There were general murmurs in the affirmative so he gingerly leaned back against the canopy and closed his eyes for a second, as if to recall her image, then went on.

115

'Yes, we were young. I must have been about nineteen at the time, so she would have been twenty, going on twenty-one. I was only in the camp a few months but we became lovers. You tend to move fast in those situations. Anyway, her tour was up and she was rotated back to London. I tried to get back on my own steam. I didn't have much money to hand but made it to Anatolia on the Mediterranean coast. I planned to cross over to Cyprus and return to the UK with the tourists. But I was out of cash I used my credit card to buy a ticket on a flight to Erkan. The Turkish MPs were waiting for me at the airport and they threw me in one of their military prisons until I could be transferred to the UK. That place made the refugee camp seem like Club Med. I was relieved when they came and got me two weeks later.

'A quick court marshal and I was packed off to the Glasshouse at Colchester. I could have done up to five years for desertion but Jenny intervened, telling them in a letter how I had helped with voluntary work and they gave me six months then threw me out.

'Is that when you married?' Julia looked pointedly at the gold band, permanently etched into his finger, 'You did marry her didn't you?'

'No and yes . . . by the time I came out, Jenny had been posted to Somalia. I had no work . . . no one wants a squadie with a dishonourable discharge on his papers. I drifted a bit, spending my benefit money on booze; eventually I took to doing the odd burglary. I was quite successful for a time, then picked the wrong house. I thought it was empty until a little old lady bashed me over the head with a brass candlestick while I was going through her jewellery box. When I

116

came to, she was phoning the police. I could have knocked her over and run for it but she reminded me of my Gran. She looked pretty frail and I didn't want to risk hurting her. I quite admired the game old bird, the way she sneaked out of bed without a sound and clocked me one. When the police arrived, we were chatting over a cup of tea in her kitchen. I went quietly. Got three years for that. The old girl even came to see me in prison.

'So how did you get into banking with a record like that?' Ted looked questioningly at the still dapper man that bore no resemblance to his delinquent past.

'I have prison to thank for that . . . It was a proper education in more ways than one. I was a bit of a wretch at first. I missed the booze. But you sober up fast inside. Especially when a smart mouth gets you a kicking from some of the other inmates. That gave me a spell in the hospital wing. After that, I shared a cell with a con man called David, for the rest of my stretch. I didn't like him at first but he knew the ways to get by. He told me that if I took to the education programme, it got me many privileges and it did. At his suggestion, I studied English and economics, did all right too. In the evenings, God the evenings are so long inside, he taught me about the confidence game. So when I came out, I was ready for a new carrier.

'But banking . . .'

'For a man with my newly found talents, it was either that or politics, and there's more money in banking.

Ted was still not convinced, 'Are you saying they just gave you a job in a bank?'

'Not a bank, Ted, "Banking," there's a big difference. What I learned was it's all about confidence, You know that, Ted, you're the same.

'In my case I just presented myself as Major Adam Stone. Recently back from the Middle East, working for British interests but the official secrets act forbids me from saying more. Slight limp from a war wound, taking early retirement with a modest pension but looking for a new challenge. A couple of forged documents and I was in. Banking is like gambling really, but with someone else's money. Easy.

'So how did you get together with Jennifer?' Julia sounded like she was getting a little impatient.

'Jenny came to see me a few times in prison. When she was home on leave. I told her about the courses I was doing, not the night school with David of course. She encouraged me and promised she would be there when I came out. True to her word, she met me at the prison gate.'

'And that is when you got back together?' Franny asked.

'Not exactly. She was living with someone else at the time. I don't think it was going too well though. She found me a bedsit in North London, I stayed there while I finish my degree and perfected my cover story. When I landed my job as a bond dealer with Allied Investment Bank, I moved up into a flat in Canary Wharf, handy for work.

'We wrote often but I didn't see her again until she turned up at a charity do I was attending as part of my new persona. She had been away, pouring her compassion into another war torn community, but had decided she had had enough. There is only so much a person can take.

'We dated a bit, while I learnt the ropes of hedge fund management, and, do you know, I was good at it. You have to be ruthless in banking and I was up to a point. Eventually I asked Jenny to marry me and, to my surprise, she said yes.'

'Ah, that is sweet,' said Julia absently.'

'Was Jennifer on the ship with you? Did she make it to a lifeboat?' Franny was suddenly concerned.

'Unfortunately I was travelling alone.' It was as if a cloud had crossed his face.

'Divorced?' Julia asked.

'Yes, divorce. My wife and my children are in Miri, that's a village in Sarawak, Malaysia. Jenny is leading the crusade to save the rainforest or something.'

'You have children too. What happened?' Franny asked, 'You obviously still love her.'

Adam reached into his jacket pocket, brought out a battered leather wallet and opened it. 'Here, that's them; it was taken just after we moved into an old priory in Kent. That's it in the background'

Franny took the wallet to look at the picture in its plastic holder. 'What a lovely house, she said. 'And lovely children too, How old are they?' She passed it on to Julia.

'Lucy's seven and Tom's five, well he was only four when that was taken. His birthday was the next day. It's Lucy's tenth next month. We always had a party for the kids. I was going to go out and surprise her.' His eyes welled up, 'I suppose I'll miss it now.'

'Don't worry, this might be all over by then.' Julia's voice carried more conviction than she felt. 'Your wife is lovely too.'

'Yes, that's my Jen.' He took the wallet back and looked lovingly at the picture. 'Happier times.'

Relieved that no one was pressing for more details, he slumped down, closed his eyes and tried to sleep.

Chapter 10

The sea was building; still a long rolling swell, but higher. After the almost flat calm of the previous day, a general sense of trepidation built within the incumbents.

The Teenager's Tale

Jenni, sensing that the others were becoming as nervous as she was, gamely tried to stimulate some conversation. Franny was particularly pale so it was to her that she said, 'And what about you young lady. Tell us how you came to be sailing with this crowd, hardly your age group, eh?'

Yes, come on, let's see what you're made of,' Adam demanded.

The young girl raised her head and fixed the man opposite with her pale turquoise eyes. The thrust of her determined little chin belying the fear in them.

'I guess you must have been travelling with someone?' Jenni once again had to diffuse the situation.

'Yes, my aunt.' Franny's voice was barely audible above the sounds of the lapping waves against the sides of the life raft.

'Why did it take so long to get you to a boat, that's what I would like to know?' Julia demanded.

Thrusting her chin even higher, the girl replied, 'I couldn't find my aunt anywhere. I still don't know where she is.' There was a catch in her voice and she gazed back at the raft's floor.

'I'm sure she's quite safe, Ted reassured her. 'The ship was well equipped with safety equipment we even have plenty of rations to see this out.'

'I hope you're right,' she continued, 'about being safe I mean. I can't believe we've sunk in the Bermuda Triangle. I found a book about it, at my aunty's. I read it all as we were going to be sailing through it. Things used to disappear here; boats, planes, people. Don't you think that's beyond weird?'

'It is certainly nothing to worry your pretty little head about, my dear. Anything spooky would take one look at my craggy old face and run for the hills.'

For the first time, Ted was rewarded with a smile.

'Now, Franny, if I may call you that?'

She nodded.

'Where do you call home?'

'I don't really have one . . . no that's not fair. I'm living with my aunt, Aunty Joyce, that is. My mom's older sister but, well, it doesn't really feel like home yet.' The words came out in a rush and Franny blushed. 'She took me in six months ago. I mean she's really kind. I've always thought she was wicked, a real laugh,' she shrugged, 'but she's not Mom.'

By now several passengers surrounding Franny were looking at her with interest and undisguised sympathy.

'Oh, you poor child.' The woman nearest her patted Franny's hand gently.

Francesca shot her a smile that did not quite reach her eyes. *I just love being treated like a child.*

She would rather have been banned from using Facebook and her I-Pad for a month than admit that, at the moment she felt like the first day she had stood at the school gate. Five years old, small and terrified. Only then, her mom had been holding her hand. God, she felt so alone. Where the hell was Aunty Joyce? Before she betrayed herself by shedding the tears that were threatening to fall, someone further down the boat was at the insistence of the others telling his tale.

She slumped into the side of the raft, which was now rocking unnervingly, hugging her blanket and misery to herself. She must look a fright, her new dress was ruined, and she could feel her auburn hair drying back into the familiar riot of curls. An hour she'd spent straightening it and all for what; and she felt hungry and sick in equal measure. Thank goodness she'd been given another seasickness pill. How awful if she threw up. That had been her first reality check. Franny hated pills and always dreaded being bad. They always seemed to get stuck in her throat or melt on her tongue. Her mom had always been there, reminding her to pop it to the back of her mouth and keep drinking and swallowing. She had begun to master the technique on the rare occasions they had been needed. But here, a while ago, it had been a different matter altogether. Knowing water was rationed hadn't helped. Franny had panicked when she had seen how little water she got to complete the task and had frozen. That had been the first time she had really noticed her smiling man.

Ted had, in a voice louder now she realised on further acquaintance, than his normal speech said, 'I used to put my pills on bread and butter and try to swallow them that way. Now of course, being a little older,' Ted had grinned widely, 'I remember to stick them right at the back of my tongue and swallow normally as I drink. Just as long as you don't panic, it seems OK.'

The wet fibres scratched against her hands and neck as she snuggled as deeply as she could into the woollen evening shawl wrapped around her slender frame. While she huddled, she wished she could disappear.

The adults were leaving her alone again at the moment, thank goodness. She sat quietly, peeking at her companions from under long eyelashes. She liked Ted, she had decided; he was nice. He reminded her of Granddad Morton. He was kind and gentle too. He lived on an old people's complex now with a warden and everything, since Granny had died. He was seventy-three, but he was still sprightly, and a real laugh. She felt a pang of sudden sadness. She loved him to bits. Wait until he heard about her adventure. Her thought drifted to her traumatic departure from the luxurious ocean.

She had been waiting patiently by the dining room doorway. Her aunty had forgotten to put her pills into her evening bag and had hurriedly returned to their cabin. Franny had offered to go back for her but "I'll be quicker; I know where they are" had been her parting shot. Now all hell was breaking loose around Franny and Joyce had been gone ages. She had no idea what she should do. Her stomach was heaving and she barely managed to step aside quickly enough as people began leaving the dining area, already starting to push and jostle each other in their haste. The sound of an incessant alarm all down the corridor was now drowning out the mournful noise of the foghorn that had been their companion for the last hour or so.

That loud bang and the way the ship had lurched must have been something serious then, she thought. Now, determined to spend not one moment longer standing there she set off at full pelt towards their cabin, not really sure of the best way to go. Skidding around a corner, she had nearly collided with one of the stewards.

'Good heavens, you shouldn't be here young lady; we are evacuating.'

'I need to find my aunt,' exclaimed Franny.

'There's no-one here; they've all been sent up to the deck. Come on, I'll take you but we must hurry.'

She had little time to catch her breath before she was in a life jacket, in the air and in the water. When she had finally been lifted into this bobbing nightmare, she had lost her aunty, her dignity and her mobile.

'So, how come you were on the ship?' asked a persistent female voice, disturbing Franny's reverie, and she certainly wasn't going to share those moments.

'Sorry, what?' Franny blinked at the woman as if seeing her for the first time.

'I asked why you were travelling from Fort Lauderdale.' Jenni persisted.

Ted kindly looked about to interrupt.

Franny mouthed to him, 'It's OK', and replied. 'My aunty is eight years older than my mom and my cousin Thomas, her only son, is a lot older than me; about twelve years to be precise. He lives there and as he was celebrating his twenty-seventh birthday, my aunt thought a trip to see him would cheer us both up.

She misses Mom a lot too. Mom and my dad were killed in a car smash, you see. My dad travelled a lot on business, so it's easier to pretend he's just away . . . Mom was always there . . . always.'

'You don't have to do this, Franny,' said a concerned Ted.

She rallied, characteristically thrust out her determined little chin and continued, 'She was right of course. It did cheer us up. Thomas made such a fuss of us. He has a beautiful apartment and you can walk to the sea; it's the Atlantic there you know. I'm not really sure I liked the place that much. Too many large hotels and high buildings but that's what America's like, I suppose.' She paused. A smile flitted across her face.

'My favourite times were walking along the paths by the sea listening to the waves lapping, or walking along the beaches, just chilling and chatting. I couldn't believe Thomas treated me like an equal, an adult. I am . . . quite but, well, usually . . . I mean. I know he's my cousin and all but it was wicked to watch all the stares he got from older girls. He's a doctor, very clever, did I tell you that, and he was with me and talking away to me . . . and he's so handsome . . .'

Realising she had exposed herself, Franny blushed and her voice trailed away. 'He's kind too,' she mumbled, seeking solace once more in the warm embrace of her wrap.

'Tell us about your parents; it's good to talk.' The woman from before demanded.

Would she never give up? God, her voice was annoying.

126

Franny lifted her head reluctantly. For anyone who had really known her, they would have seen the defiant flash in her sad turquoise eyes. Still, it would take her mind off things. 'Since you're so interested.' Francesca checked herself; she could hear her mother's voice telling her rudeness was not becoming and took a deep breath, calming herself and the desire in her head to scream, "leave me alone!"

'You said your father travelled a lot. What did he do?'

'He worked for an oil company. He was an expert on oil pipelines; whatever that means. Dad actually grew up in America. Granddad and Granny Morton emigrated there when he was about ten, I think. My mom met him out there. She was a research chemist for the same company. She was adventurous, my mom,' she sighed 'she'd probably think this was fun. I think she must have wanted excitement and to see the world. Not like Nan and Grandpa Ellis. They've never moved. They're in the same house they've been in since their twenties.' Her voice rose, incredulously.

All the while Francesca had been speaking she had been toying with her earrings, which had thankfully survived her undignified leap.

They're pretty studs,' a female voice remarked.

Franny gulped, 'They were dad's last gift. Sometimes he'd be away for days, weeks, but he always came back with, "gifts for his two bestest girls." She smiled as the memory flitted across her mind. 'He'd stand by us, whip out the presents from behind his back and go "da da, the awards tonight go to . . . " My mom said he was clearly a frustrated showman, Franny giggled, but I know she loved it really. I used to get DVD's, CD's, books, I adore books. This time it was different.' Visible, naked pain swept across her gentle young face. 'They're Swarovski, my earrings. Dad said I was too young for diamonds but that he could see I was a young woman now and every woman deserved things as beautiful as they were.' She blushed slightly.

'They were his last gift,' she repeated. By now she was sobbing. The woman nearest made as if to reach out to her. Francesca shook her head and turned her face to the interminable sea.

Chapter 11

As the day wore on, the sun hazed over a little and an increase in humidity added to the discomfort of the closely packed occupants of the floating rubber prison. There was no shortage of lookouts trying to relieve the sticky boredom of the covered enclosure.

The Waiter's Tale

Caz was taking a turn as the official lookout, 'If you can see birds on the horizon, does that mean there is land?

'Only if they are ostriches,' the waiter laughed as he eased himself out of the hatch alongside her. 'Can you see some?'

'Well, only one actually,' she pointed at the distant spec.

'It's probably an albatross. They spend most of their lives at sea, far from anywhere, and only land to breed.' Tony winced as he slid himself back inside, the other survivors were looking at him expectantly. 'False alarm,' he said, 'the sea's as empty as a nuns date book,' he grinned. 'I did have a close encounter with an albatross once though.'

'When was that?'

'Oh, it must have been about seventeen or eighteen years ago now, I suppose. I'd signed up as winch-man on an ocean racer. We were in the lead in the Whitbread . . .'

'The Whitbread?' Clarissa queried.

'Yeah, you know, the round the world yacht race. Well, we were dis-masted and had to drift around for days, waiting for a tow. I was on watch one night; crouching in the cockpit, freezing my nuts off and trying not to fall asleep. We were much further south, than we are now, heading for the Cape. The wind had dropped to nothing, not as still as this but very light and we were in a long slow swell. The sea looked like pewter in the moonlight and the sky was inky black but filled with stars. As a matter of fact, last night reminded me of exactly that. We were all exhausted and glad of the calm for a while, but were getting bored by then.

'Anyway, I suddenly had this feeling that I was not alone. I had the hood up on my dry suit so just swivelled my eyes towards a light patch at the edge of my vision, to find another beady little eye staring straight back at me. It was an albatross. You wouldn't believe how big they are close up. It wasn't perched, you understand, it was flying; well, floating on the air actually. Its wing tip almost brushed the side of our boat but its head was a good five feet further away. It seemed to just hover there, effortlessly. No flapping or anything, just letting the light breeze hold it a few feet above the swell. We sat there regarding each other for all of five minutes. I daren't move in case I scared it off; it was just so beautiful, in a majestic sort of way. Mind you, its beak looked quite fierce with a sharp hook on the end. I began to wonder if it was looking at me as a fellow seafarer or a source of food. In the end, I risked turning my head to get a better look. I was so aware of the rustling of the fabric of my suit. But it wasn't fussed, it just turned its head my way too, looking aloof and defiant. Eventually, it drifted a bit further away and, without any perceptible wing movements, made a slow circuit of the boat. Then it faded away into the night, skimming the waves until lost from sight. There was a tear in my eye when it was gone, I don't mind admitting.

'So' Ted asked 'how come you were dis-masted, then?'

'Ah that's another story, do you want to hear it?

'Go on then, we've got nothing else better to do,' said DJ, settling in his seat.

'Well, as I said, we were in the Whitbread. It's called the Volvo now; the name changes with the main sponsor. So I was crew, signed up for my muscle rather than brains. Dave Barratt, our skipper, was well known in ocean racing circles, notorious for pushing hard, but on this occasion, he pushed too hard. There were ten in the crew; Dave and his strategist were experienced racers; I was on as an experienced spare, but the other seven oiks had never raced before. Five of the guys were from a rugby team, fearless to the point of insanity, with total faith in the skipper. I, on the other hand, coming from a long line of fishermen, had more respect for the sea and, if not actually scared at that time, was beginning to get nervous. We had crossed the Atlantic no problem and were heading into the Southern ocean. There was a huge swell and storm force winds. Waves had overhanging crests with spray whipping off them. The sea was milky with foam and some of the waves started breaking into the cockpit. It was about time to shorten sail but as long as we were close hauled — that is sailing as close to the wind as possible — we were ok. Those yachts are built for just that kind of weather.

'On deck, we were all clipped on and wearing our dry suits. The spray on our faces felt more as if we were being lashed with a miniature cat-o-nine-tails though. Half the time we had our eyes shut. But in teams of two on the big winches we had to crank for all we were worth, first in one direction and then in the other, just to keep the sails in trim as we climbed up one side of a wave and pitched headlong down the other. We had been doing this for hours and I, for one, was exhausted. I'm not a small man but our rugby-playing gorillas called me Titch. Strangely enough, the biggest of them was a second row forward of nineteen stone, they called Tiny. He was my mate on the winch to compensate for my comparative weakness. Even with the gale shrieking in our ears we could hear, or more like feel, the rigging humming like a piano on sustain.

'I still can't be sure what happened but, with a sound like a gunshot, one of the shrouds snapped setting off a chain reaction as one by one the mainstays came under more pressure and parted. The carbon fibre mast creaked and groaned then shattered, broken off just above the deck. The whole rig sails and everything went over the side. Trailing cables whipped about all over the deck. One guy was swept over the side and was being dragged along held by his lanyard. Of course, we were all off our feet and scrabbling about, it was like an overturned henhouse. It's a miracle no one was killed right there and then. Waves were pitching into the outstretched mainsail threatening to turn the boat over we had to cut away the remaining cables and ditch the rig before it pulled us under.

'I knew this from tales my father had told me, but I didn't have the strength left in me to do it alone. I screamed at Tiny. He looked at me blankly for what seemed like an age before he understood what we had to do. There is a set of bolt croppers in a pocket on these boats for just that purpose. I made for it.

You have two lanyards on your harness so you can hook one on another anchorage before you take the first one off. It took two re-hooks to get there from where I was. I grabbed the croppers and turned round. Tiny was right behind me. I could see both of his lanyards dangling free. He clung to a winch with one hand and reached out for the cutter with the other. Waves were crashing into the deck, washing our feet from under us. But he was planted there and I was on my arse at his feet. The main cable we needed to cut was about ten feet away. I handed him the tool then grabbed the swinging end of his tether. As he turned, I hooked it on to the safety cable that runs around the deck, and pointed at where he had to cut. He kind of forward rolled away passing straight through a wall of green water. I got up and tried to follow but couldn't keep upright. By the time I got reoriented, he was already at the cable. One chomp and it was free and luckily, the two remaining minor shrouds parted of their own accord. Now we were just a hull, bobbing like a cork in a Jacuzzi, but we were able to get everyone sorted out. We dragged the man in from over the side and the skipper, who probably had concussion because he had a deep cut on his head, managed to set off the automatic distress beacon before passing out.

Apart from that, we had one man with a broken arm and the rest of us mostly bruises and minor cuts. We hunkered down in the sail locker and rode out the storm. An uncomfortable twenty-four-hours, I can tell you. Eventually the sea died down and all we had to do was wait. That was when I had the encounter with the albatross. We were picked up by a South African war ship four days later.

Tony looked around at the nervous faces and grinned. 'With modern technology and communications, no one is completely lost at sea for long. Even now, some satellite is picking up the locator signal from our Epirb and has a fix on us. It is just a matter of waiting for a ship to come along.

We will probably see a coastguard aircraft first. Maybe a helicopter or flying boat. We'll be fine, just relax and enjoy the ride.

'What's an Epurb?' asked Franny, 'sounds a bit purvey to me.'

'E-P-I-R-B . . . Emergency Position Indicating Radio Beacon. If it is the type with GPS, they know where we are to within 50 metres.

'If you had such a bad experience, how come you chose to work as a waiter on a cruise ship?' Franny asked, 'I would have thought you would have wanted to stay on land after that.'

'On the contrary . . . Tony shifted his weight, grimacing and holding his ribs. 'I love the sea.' Settling more comfortably he grinned 'I did say that I came from a long line of fishermen. As a matter of fact, if I had my way as a kid I would have followed my father into the family business. We owned our own small trawler out of Arbroath. Danny, my older brother, skippers her now and my kid sister helps mum run our smoking business. You've heard of Arbroath Smokies? Hot smoked Haddock, I was brought up on it, although I only eat it now when my mum sends me some from home.

'Ah, a boy and his mum eh?' Caz commented

'Well, I wanted to be a fisherman too. In the school holidays, we used to go out with Dad and I loved it. But my mother came from Italy and was mad about education. She insisted I stay on at school and go to college. She didn't care what I studied, just as long as I got a degree. So I took a BSG, expecting to go back and partner my brother, maybe get another boat. But while I was away in Edinburgh, things changed in the fishing industry. Quotas and big foreign trawlers hoovering up the shoals made it harder to sustain the amount of boats as they were; let alone run a new one. Many a skipper bailed out. There were plenty of boats going cheap but they all needed a lot of work to keep sea worthy. Mum must have seen it coming, I suppose. I was still at Uni when Dad died. Heart attack. I wanted to come home straight away and help Danny but Mum insisted I finish the course. Eventually I did join the crew but Danny was like our old man, worse really, as a skipper. We fought all the time we were at sea. He was great as a brother though. He found me my first yacht crew job. I travelled a bit, crewing for wealthy owners moving their million pound cruisers around the world. I studied up for my Yacht-Master and DOT commercial skipper's ticket between trips and took all the racing slots I could find. I did the "Round Britain" and the "Fasnet" then I got the chance in the Whitbread.

'After that, I found a sponsor for my own racer. But, to be honest, I wasn't as successful as I'd hoped. I won at Cowes a few times and skippered for Nike in the Mediterranean Cup but, in the great racing challenges, I was way off the pace. Not brave enough, or is it mad enough. Anyway, I did complete the round the world, dead last, but at least we came back in one piece. Once you do that well-paid jobs start to roll in and, eventually, I was able to buy a big cruising catamaran and took up skippered chartering. Made a good life in Florida.'

Sadness crept past the premature crow's feet on his tanned face into his dark brown eyes. 'I had this cruising cat. An Atlantic 57, she was beautiful.

'I used to take rich Americans out from the Keys for a few nights on board, some snorkelling, spear fishing you know the sort of thing. It was a great life. '

'If all that's true, how come you are working as a waiter now?'DJ asked

'That was all Irene's fault.'

'Irene?'

'Hurricane Irene. Last August.' Tony smiled a sad smile. I had flown back to Scotland to see my Mother. She was ill in hospital. It was the eighteenth when I got the call. I had a party of five on board the Lucy-Tania, that was the name of my boat. A couple who had sailed with me before and their friends, a family of three. Mum, Dad and a snotty nosed kid of about six; they were strictly landlubbers. I explained my problem and the Wilsons were very sympathetic. I offered them their money back, or to get them another charter, but the Andrettis kicked up a fuss. They were paying over a thousand bucks a day and their little

Johnny wanted to be a pirate, RIGHT NOW. Well I knew Bill and Dawn Wilson were competent sailors, so I let them take the others out. I told them to cruise in the Gulf for a few days while I was away and I would take them along the Keys when I got back.

'I was in Arbroath a couple of days later, when the first signs of a tropical storm blew up. I watched the met reports on my laptop, sweating it out at my Mums bedside. She'd had a stroke but was recovering by then. I chatted to Bill on the satellite phone. I told him to stay deep in the Gulf and then headed back as best I could. I had to fly to New York and got there just before Irene closed the Airport. I could not raise the Lucy but from the hurricanes track, along the Atlantic coast, I figured they would be all right in the gulf. By the time I got back to the Keys, my clients were all in a hotel and my beloved Lucy was at the bottom of the sea.

'It transpired that, as soon as the sea started to get a bit lumpy, the kid got seasick and the Andretti's panicked. They insisted that Bill took them back which, of course, was straight into the path of the storm. Lucy was swamped and they had to call the coastguard to take them off.

'Wasn't your boat insured then?' Caz asked

'For them waters it was virtually impossible to insure the boat itself. I had cover for passengers and their luggage, etcetera, but as it transpired, the small print excludes going to sea without me on board. The Wilsons were good as gold about it but their so-called friends were out for blood. They sued everyone in sight: Bill, for incompetence in charge of the vessel, me for everything from abandoning a vessel in danger to operating a vessel unfit for its purpose. They even sued the US met office and the coastguard for failing to inform them of the danger.

'Of course the lawyers settled, so here I am pot-less. Worse than that, I have a million dollar debt for their costs. I tried to work ashore but hated it. There's nothing going at home and I am too old at forty-two to get back on the racing circuit so, to give myself a break, I work the cruise ships just to be on the sea.

'Now, if someone would like to sponsor me, I could put together another charter business.' He shot a sideways glance at Caz, not here again, but maybe in the Med. There is still money to be made.'

Chapter 12

Tony sniffed the air. His fisherman's instinct warned of a change in the weather. The horizon on a clear day is about four and a half kilometres from the top of the raft but he calculated that visibility was less than three. Not significant for the many eyes that scanned for rescue but, to high flying aircraft and passing shipping, their diminutive craft, bright orange though it was, could easily be lost in the murk. But that in itself was not his main concern. He decided to wait before voicing his concerns. The weather in this part of the world changed quickly and the next hour or two would prove significant.

The Dancer's Tale

Ken and Dianna, despite their shaky start found an affinity with each other and as evening made its rapid advance they settled down alongside one another to talk.

'So, you never did tell me how you came to be on this particular cruise,' Ken said, softly.

'Well . . . I wasn't first choice. Linda, a friend of mine and a dancer like me, was booked. She twisted her ankle (a common injury in my profession). She asked me to take her place. Actually, I was between shows and just finished the Costa line out of the

Caribbean and Nassau. To be honest I needed a rest, but I needed the money too. So I took the job.'

'But how did you become a dancer in the first place?'

'Ah, well; when I was a wee girl, *me* mammy and Dervla my older sister, watched a film on video, "The Red Shoes," with Moira Shearer the ballet dancer. That was it for me. I knew all I ever wanted to do was dance. Any kind of dancing was like a dream for me to watch. Oh . . . those ballroom couples looking as if they were gliding through the clouds; dream people I used to say. Then Mammy took me, Dervla, and Francis my brother, to Agnes O'Brien's school for Irish dancing. To start with just to see if it was a passing phase with us. It wasn't, I was hooked. 'Jesus, I remember Agnes putting a stick behind me back to keep it straight for many gruelling years. At the competitions, all the deep blues, reds, greens, and swirling Celt designs on the costumes and glittering broaches, resembling little fairies without wings. The unison of steps in line, the sound of heavy flared brocade and the squelching of patent leather on wooden floors, from hornpipe shoes. Jesus you got warm in those outfits.

Dervla was more into ballroom since she had a book *Da* bought her one Christmas. But she stuck to the Irish because we could be together, and after her lesson she could meet with Sean Cassidy, the local heart throb, and his group They were called the 'The Islanders'. So I was her alibi too!

Our Francis was at the age when it wasn't thought to be cool to be dancing in a skirt. Most of his friends laughed at him, so he decided it wasn't for him. Until he met Kathleen O'Malley there who he fancied like mad. She soon changed his mind so the dancing was OK for a while. Then, after a few months, it was over and he started going all holy. I mean really holy, blessing himself all the time. It was like living with St Patrick; you had to watch every word you said. Always following father Loran around after mass. I know he was an altar boy but still he seemed obsessed. Not surprisingly, he became a priest.

Looking back, I thought he might have been, you know . . . gay, and with all that abuse they say happened. I don't think it did to Francis.

'Jesus, Mary and Joseph,' she muttered, blessing herself before going on. 'If there had been any impropriety, my brother would've punched him one, priest or no priest, he doesn't have red hair for nothing.

'After attaining many medals and trophies for Irish dancing at feish's and khaelis, I wanted more scope with dancing so I trained in ballet and tap. "I'm a bow legged chicken and a knock kneed hen, never been so happy since I don't know when, I walk with a wiggle and a giggle and a squawk, doing the Tennessee wig walk." Sorry about that, I couldn't resist it, my very first tap routine. Years later I went to train in Latin and Ballroom. So, despite what you see, this,' she said, gesturing to herself proudly, 'beneath the carnival of superficiality, is a very accomplished dancer.'

'I realise that already,' Ken said kindly.

'I can remember *Da* watching us all, me, Dervla, and Francis, as we practised our heavy jigs in the school playground. He just looked, never came over to us. On a few occasions he actually made an attendance to watch us dance at some competition, he'd always stand at the back of the crowds, away from any would be accusations and discriminations. I think he wanted to be different, to be closer to us, but knew he couldn't change, couldn't help himself. I got to thinking, it's a shame he was a drifter, a maverick, but a drink was never far away and it will always remain his first love.

'I think that's why I went for older men, because I never had a father around to look up to.'

Isobel, who had been listening intently to their conversation from the position directly opposite asked, 'Did you ever go out with any one famous? Don't spare us any juicy bits!' Diana looked up at her questioner then shot a glance at Jenni. 'Well yes . . .'

'Go on, go on, don't stop now,' Jenni said, gesturing with her hand to continue.

'There was an actor, very well-known, from East Enders, who had come on one the cruises to get away from the media . . . And an ITV producer, who came on to me at an end of show party in the West End. And once I was proposed to by a Saudi Prince, who owned a football club and cruise liners.

'No, I can't continue. Put it this way, I have used and they have used, well them more than me, because I gained nothing. I'm not going to name names, but there have been many'.

'Why not, we won't tell will we?' Isobel incited support from the others.

'No, if you don't mind.'

'What a pity, I love a bit of celeb gossip,' Clarissa chimed in, 'Do tell us about anybody else interesting you have met?'

'OK, Well . . . On an Apollo Line cruise around the Greek islands, I met a very kind old gentleman who had recently lost his wife to cancer. There was nothing like that . . . if that's what you're thinking. He just wanted to talk to me; a lot of people seem to. Anyway, because I listened and had a couple of dances, because he looked so lonely, he offered me money, not for that . . . but he said he was so grateful that a young woman like me took the time to care about him. I refused the money. We kept in touch after the cruise and he still writes to me even now. I think I'm the granddaughter he never had, and he is the granddad I never had. I've met so many big names, but it's the stalwarts of the working classes that come on these cruises, with their own personal losses and remaining steadfast, like sturdy ships, or life's soldiers with dignity and duty that I love the most to entertain. Happy with their lot, they don't expect any more or less. It's these ordinary folk that impress me. They are the real important people not Dukes, Duchesses, aristocrats. Does that surprise you?

'I know I'm ambitious but this is the truth. To me they have no soul, no sense of reality and honour, and most of them I've met are nasty, arrogant and inhumane. And I know I speak for most of the crew here, that we are basically down to earth people, earning money on the cruises to better our lives, and seeing the world at the same time of course.'

'Yes, we know that you see the world,' Isobel said, 'and also see a lot of each other, so I've been told.'

'Oh you mean sex!' Diana grinned. 'Oh Jesus, we're at it all the time. But so is every other industry, the airline crews are rampant to be sure. Its show business; it'll never change. I've found a few people in compromising situations, I can tell you. Not actually celebs, but friends of mine.

'Oh, do tell, I'm all ears.'

'Well, seeing as you don't know the people or person involved I suppose it's alright. I was working in London on this occasion at some charity "Variety Show of Great Britain". Me and my sister were magician's assistants that night as well, and doves were flying all around the dressing room. Then later, with some other dancers, we had to share a dressing room with an impressionist/vocalist. He was a good looking guy on stage. However, off stage, he took of his toupee, completely bald, then a truncheon from the front of his trousers, do you know that pop groups do that too! Then, off come his high platform shoes, without fake tan, he was as pale as milk. Then to top it all false teeth. I do have another similar anecdote if you want to hear?'

'I'm all ears.'

'A friend of mine called Freddie, who I met when I auditioned for the Royal Ballet. I was accepted but it was made clear that I would never be another Darcy Bussell. At that moment, with the disappointment of it all, I felt more like Dawn French in the mirror routine that they performed together in the Vicar of Dibley. Ha-ha.

Anyway, Freddie was a comedian working the London night clubs circuits, and was also a reporter doing reviews on the shows in the West End. Many years later, he came to work on the latest cruise I was on, the Sigma Star Lines, from Felixstowe to cruise all around Scandinavia. Well, to hurry the story along, he became friendly with one of the passengers, an attractive Swedish woman who looked to be in her forties. This particular night they had been watching the cabaret, from a table near the stage where I was dancing. After my slot, I changed, and noticed they had gone. However, the woman had left her clasp purse bag on the chair next to where she had been sitting. I collected it and, having located the cabin where Frankie was staying, knocked on the door.

"'Just a minute." he said, and opened the door wearing only his robe. I looked over his shoulder and could see the woman in bed with sparse tufts of hair, beside her on the table was her wig and her dentures in a jar. I swear I don't know how I didn't laugh in his face, it was very difficult. Jesus, she looked like his mother! Freddie was thirty eight. He told me later that the room had been in darkness until I knocked on the door. Whether that's the truth or not, I'll never know. Towhee, I never let him forget it. But he sort of got his own back on me several years later. When me and my beautiful brunette sister, who looked like Jaclyn Smith of Charlie's Angels, and Freddie were going into a night club in Manchester, I was walking a few paces behind Freddie and my sis but they were talking to the club bouncer who, apparently, Freddie knew. Unknown to me Freddie had said one of the girls is a singer/dancer the other one a stripper. As I walked down the steps all three of them were looking at me. The bouncer was actually ogling me. I asked Freddie, What he had said to him on the door. He told me, and Dervla had quickly added, "and I'm the singer."So there you have it. Sadly, Freddie, and my sister are gone now. Both buried in the same cemetery, not far from each other.' Diana's eyes filled with tears. 'I have no Mammy, no *da* and no sister. I'm an orphan. There's me brother Francis, of course, who I see from time to time. But I miss my big sis . . . She wiped her tears and nose with the sleeve of her dress. 'It's left me permanently devastated, losing my family, my mammy, and sister. Part of you stays dead with them, doesn't it? I know it sounds silly, but I feel their presence. I sense it helping me, that's my only comfort.'

'There is another member of my family who is absolutely adorable, and who I miss so very much; 'That's my Charlie, my darling Charlie.' Diana tried to hold back the tears. 'My son.'

'Well, aren't you the dark horse,' Jenni said, 'I had no idea after all this time and all the chats we've had, why didn't you tell me?'

'Let's face it . . . it's not the sort of thing I want to brag about and get around the crew. Would you?'

'No, I suppose not. Where is he?'

'In Ireland with my auntie Kathleen. I send money that I earn from the cruises I work on into her bank account in Ireland. He'll be five in March coming, my little babe, my fairy child. Well, I've told you that much, might as well tell you the rest. I went to Dublin to dance for a couple of nights in Riverdance.'

'You performed in Riverdance! That's impressive interjected Ken.

'Yeah, told you I'm good. I've also got a bit of a brain too, contrary to what is said about blondes. After working in the show I studied for a history degree at Trinity College, Dublin. On an Open University Course, part time. I have 'O' levels and 'A' levels and was lucky they accepted me. I swear to God it was just like Educating Rita, that room and the bloody sticky door. I expected Michael Caine to be sat behind the desk, which I wouldn't have minded one bit. Anyway, my tutor was called Gerry Fitzpatrick and a total contrast to the whisky slugging academic. He was tee total and looked like the actor 'Rufus Sewell'. Need I say any more? I could've made something of my life, instead of this, but I let sex get in the way. I didn't complete the course, fell hopelessly in love with him and had a short passionate affair. Charlie is a result of my sin if you like, but I wouldn't change him for the world. Sounds perfect doesn't it? The only problem was Gerry was married, his wife was an intensely religious woman. Ever see the film Carrie and her fanatical mother. Need I say more? So there you have it from the whore of Babylon, or Delilah as she calls me. Had no children; sex was out! Not what she expected really. She can think what she likes of me but don't take it out on my son. She won't have him at their house as he is a constant reminder of Gerry's betrayal. So Gerry goes to see him at aunt Kathleen's every week.

'Do you see Charlie when you return to Ireland?' Isobel asked. 'It seems such a shame that you don't see him. Would you like to settle down one day?'

'There is nothing I want more than to have Charlie with me for good. That's why I work the cruise ships, to a save as much as I can. As for settling down, I would love to get married, but love doesn't love me. I'm not designed to be truly happy; this is why I am the way I am. I vowed to myself I would do anything to give Charlie a good start. I have to keep working and use what assets God has given me. I do not want to end up like mammy was with *da*. She used to say, "Don't make the same mistakes I did, I want better for you all." That was a sham of a marriage never knowing when he was coming home. I've tried to turn my life around alright, one mess after another. What a fool I've been!'

'Now, now, my dear,' Isobel said, 'don't get upset, things have a way of working out.'

'My mammy used to say, "Always looks for the good in people."'

'I can agree with that,' Isobel smiled.

'She also said, "It's not a world to bring children into."'

'I wish I had listened to her words, but we all make mistakes don't we?' Diana did not wait for a response. 'She also said that people who work on boats and holiday camps are running away from something.'

She turned to her companion, who had been quiet for quite a while. 'My dad was always running away until one day he ran away for good .Don't know where and I don't care. Tell me, Mr Watts, what are you running away from?'

'I wouldn't be surprised if you see your *da* one of these days on one of the ships you're on?' Ken said by way of reply.

'Hope not,' she said between gritted teeth, 'He was a drunk; used to work on the docks. Finish work; spend all night in Shaughnessy bar. Plenty of money for mates, and Guinness, but none left for us, Mammy, me, my sister and brother. It's no wonder Francis went to be a priest. After what I've seen, it's a wonder I didn't go and take me vows at St Theresa's Covent. You can laugh at what you see before you, Ken. I'm not saying he meant to be bad, but he was. To be sure he was a handsome devil, tall with dark curly hair, and piercing blue eyes, and he had that Celt charm. He could charm any woman between the sheets, much to mammy's concern. Even the angels if he set his mind to it. Don't think they ever meant anything to him though. Not like with mammy and him. I was only a wee thing but I knew! That's why I never understood why he could hurt her so much. Oscar Wilde could never grasp why we always hurt the one we love could he?'

Ken nodded sagely and let the girl pour out her story uninterrupted.

'They met when my mammy was working at Murphy's bar in Sligo Street,' she went on, 'After six pints of Guinness he plucked up the courage to ask her out. She kept refusing but he kept on. Eventually, she succumbed to his charm. Sometimes I used to catch him dancing, that's when he wasn't drinking. At my Uncle Paddy's funeral, *Da* was praising him to high heaven oh what a great mate he was to him. Then after the bevies it was, "that bloody bastard Paddy he owes me money." That's what the drink does to you. It may bring a smile to ya face, when it's about someone else's shenanigans. But when it's close to home it's not so funny.

'He used to beat mammy, just because she was singing, or for any other reason, depends what was on his mind at the time. Can you imagine that? What she went through and what we witnessed at such a young age. Such a lovely voice she had too, it was like Sarah Brightman's from the Phantom of the Opera. Why did he hit her when she started to sing? Because his mammy used to hit him with a belt to the tune of Danny Boy, after drinking whisky. Ever since then, when he'd been on the drink, he hated any singing. My poor mammy, it was her only pleasure, singing to us and he took that away from her. Missed her way she did. Why did he turn something so beautiful into something so ugly? She used to teach singing you know. *Da* never knew. Well someone had to pay the bills, didn't they? Do you know I'm a vocalist too? I have sung on all the cruises I've worked on; this is my fourth one. I would love to sing a duet with Gareth, the Entertainment Manager before he leaves to start his new contract. But I don't think Jenni, his wife, is too keen on the idea, so I'll sing solo. Thinking about it I don't think that the choice of songs "When your bodies had enough of me, and I'm lying down there on the floor," and the other "If I said you had a beautiful body would you hold it against me" would go down very well with Jenni.'

Diana looked sincerely at Jenni and said, 'you don't know how lucky you and Gareth are to have each other I realised years ago that falling for another woman's husband is not morally right. Yes, it is my religion, my inner voice my own personal ethic that is revealing itself. I'm so sorry Jenni, you must believe me. I was getting the wrong messages from Gareth. I feel like I 'm betraying mammy if I do, as *Da* was always going off with other women.

'When Da finally left us, mammy took a job as a waitress and continued to teach singing in the evenings, bless her, while my brother used to babysit. When she came in she was dog weary, that's when we began to notice the change in her little things at first then big things. Kept forgetting where she put things and not tidying up, forgetting to cook our meals. She had a tumour; doctor said it was caused through being hit in the head over a period of time. Well, we know who caused that don't we?'

Raft of Life

Chapter 13

The swell had increased during the day and being on lookout duty became popular as the view of the horizon helped quell the nausea that even the seasickness pills couldn't quell.

A Chance of Rescue

They heard it first; a faint drone but the distant sky was shrouded in cloud. It took a while for the lookouts, straining their ears and turning their heads this way and that, to settle on a direction in which to peer hopefully into the hazy distance.

'I think I can see something, pass me the binoculars someone.' Ted pointed towards the setting sun.

'Oh yes over there, a plane. Has he seen us?' Caz tried to stand up, clinging to the canopy at the opposite lookout post. The raft rocked violently as everyone scrambled to the hatches. 'Careful you'll have me in,' she yelled.

Ted tried to focus the binoculars on the distant spec, but had to wait until the rocking abated before he could bring them to bear. 'Yes, it's a flying boat.'

'The US coastguard,' said Tony, 'I told you they would find us.'

'Is he coming this way?' Caz shaded her eyes with her free hand while the whitened knuckles of the other clutched the fabric of the roof.

'I can't tell . . . I think so . . . I can see both wings . . . better get a flare ready.'

Ken appeared at the central hatch clutching two cylinders. 'Which one shall I use?'

Jenni, her head and shoulders sticking out of the end hatch, pointed at the one with the red cap. 'That one, the parachute . . . '

'Like this?'David fumbled with the tag.

'Oh for God's sake, give it to me.' Adam scrambled across the jumble of legs to emerge alongside Ken and made to grab the flare. Ted promptly turned away and the flare fired but, instead of soaring high into the sky, it shot off sideways for about thirty feet before plunging into an oncoming wave, which it illuminated from within for a moment before being extinguished.

'Now look what you've done.' Ken snapped and ducked back inside to fetch another flare.

'Hurry up,' Ted kept his binoculars trained on their rescuer. 'They're turning away.'

Ken pulled the tag on his other flare. Although he held it at arm's length the thick, acrid, smoke wafted back on the rising wind to fill the interior of the raft.

'You idiot,' Adam choked, 'throw it into the sea before we are all asphyxiated.'

Jenni clambered through to the opposite hatch and, thrusting her hand as high as she could, fired another flare. This time it rocketed into the sky, leaving a rippling vapour trail until, with a loud pop, it burst into a miniature sun that hurt the eyes to look at. Dangling from its parachute it drifted away on its slow decent.

'Right,' Jenni shouted at the men across the canopy, 'from now on, no-one touches the flares but me and Tony . . . got it?'

The two nodded back shamefacedly while each asserting that the other was at fault.

'Have they seen it . . . have they?' Caz strained to see the distant aircraft.

'They are still turning,' Ted kept up a commentary. 'Still turning . . . they're heading away now . . . still heading away . . .'

'They're flying a search pattern, mostly looking down,' Tony said calmly from his position sitting alongside Caz. 'They're too far to the west . . . don't worry, they'll work their way over here sooner or later.'

The sun had started to set, radiating searchlight beams between the bulky mass of heavy cumulus cloud that hugged the western sky.

'No good, they're definitely going away now.' Ted said, taking the binoculars from his eye for the first time in several minutes. The aircraft was just a diminishing spec about to be swallowed by the distance.

'I think we had better get back inside and make things secure,' said Tony, I don't like the look of them thunderheads over there. What do you think Ted?'

Turney shrugged and in flat tones said, 'I think it'll rain tonight.'

'Well we can look forward to some fresh water then,' said Jenni, trying, without success, to lighten the mood. 'Come on everybody nutrient sticks and a water ration all round and don't forget to take your seasickness pills.'

One by one they rearranged themselves in the raft and secured the canvas covers on the hatchways. By the time they had finished distributing the food, the first heavy drops of rain began to thump onto the canopy. As night fell, distant thunder could be heard; the lightning flashes illuminating the canopy material and flashing through the gaps around the openings. They rose and fell with increasing violence and the rain beat a drum solo on the roof.

'Tony, I'm scared,' Caz whispered.

'It's all right,' Tony put his arm around her slender shoulders and hugged her to him. 'It'll blow itself out by morning.'

For hours, the storm raged. The wind shrieked through the gaps between the flaps of the hatches, bringing spray and rain with it. Sometimes waves splashed up the sides, forcing jets of water through the ill fitting Velcro fasteners. On one occasion, a hatch cover was ripped wide open and it took the combined efforts of Ted, Tony, Adam and Ken to struggle out into the sizzling darkness to re-secure it. At least the desperate need to work as a team diffused the animosity between the soldier and policeman.

For the most part, everyone hunkered down under the crackling foil blankets, clinging together and praying harder than ever for deliverance.

Chapter 14

As Tony had predicted the storm abated by the small hours. Once the thunder and lightning stopped most of the survivors managed to get an hour or two of sleep before dawn. They were left bobbing in a much steeper sea than before but they had come through the night safely cocooned in the battened down raft.

The Divorcee's Tale

As the sun rose, Julia looked distinctly grumpy.

'It's been some long while since I was woken at dawn by my husband leaving our bed to get to the City.' she said. 'Had to be there for the Asian markets to open . . . apparently.

'Never was my favourite time of day but now it just brings back ghastly memories. Lately, I've found it better to wake towards noon. Let the day start gradually. In any case, why on earth are we all so keen to wake up now? We have precisely nothing to do and nowhere to go. Sleep seems a far better deal. But without my trusty pills in this wretched daylight, I doubt I'll manage to nod off.'

She sank down into the lifeboat and closed her eyes. 'I've been through worse than this', she muttered to herself. The court case, which resulted in her being forced to give up her adored son, was now a benchmark she used to gauge the bouts of despair which had regularly enveloped her since her "rehabilitation", as her father insisted on describing it. She had found that the only way to survive was to hide her real self from the world and be grateful for the way Daddy had stood by her, despite the depths to which she had sunk.

She had to block all the pain and heartache, all the longing and love for her child. Sometimes, when strangers perfunctorily enquired, it seemed easier to pretend that she didn't have any children; she did not have the strength to embark on her story and, even if she did, how could anyone who had not been there understand her bitter experience?

Wearily, she surveyed the other occupants of the lifeboat. *Oh God*, she thought, *what a way to go, with these losers. Daddy must have been mad to think I would find romance and "Start A New Life" on this lousy cruise.* She was jolted from her musings by a grating Midland accent and realised with horror that it was directed at her.

'Ok, luv, wake up! Your turn.' Jenni's words would not be ignored.

Julia's initial reaction was to retreat into her shell and recite her rather boring, recently created life story to satisfy such an unwelcome intrusion. But then she was struck by a radical, daring thought. What had her psychotherapist been telling her all this time? That it could be healing to be honest and open when confidences were assured. Well, she reasoned, any confidences in this boat are guaranteed to remain such; she doubted anyone would survive the current ordeal.

She drew herself up, and took a deep breath. "Ok, great, thank you. My name is Lady Julia Pemberton and, due to my alcoholism, I have been forced to give up my husband and child. How's that for starters?'

'Whaat?' Diana gasped as she made the sign of the cross. Do you really mean you were married to a Lord?'

Julia tossed her head. 'That's the least of my problems, believe me. Anyway, let me tell you from the beginning.

'It was easy to succumb to his charms. In those days he was a handsome young man with dark hair, short but neatly cut, and astonishing blue eyes. He was not as tall as me, but at first I hadn't noticed that as he was slouched against the bar, tankard of beer in his hand, slightly apart from the rest of the crowd, yet almost as if he was apart by choice. He was superior, better. Aloof? No, that's not the right word. Anyway, he just gestured with his head as if to invite me over. Nothing else, just a brief movement of his head and my stomach lurched. Oh well, might as well wander over. Stay nonchalant, keep calm.

He waited for me to join him. "What are you drinking?" he asked.

'"Beer, please." And that was the start of my relationship with Hugh – or "Lord Pemberton," as I subsequently discovered. A stupid beer, a nod of the head, and my life was doomed to change irrevocably.

'God, you must have been an easy lay,' Ken muttered quietly.

Julia ignored him and continued. 'Little did I realise what was ahead. I'd read my horoscope that morning which sounded promising. "Gemini: Be prepared for a chance to change your whole life"

'Anyway, there's not much to say about those early carefree days. It was just typical of a Uni romance, a bit of a fling which seemed so grown up; plenty of sex, drink and partying with absolutely no responsibility. And of course, in my case there was the extra exciting bit knowing that I was going out with a man totally removed from my suburban upbringing, which made me feel that I had finally broken free from the small-minded world that Daddy inhabited. I must admit that it gave Hugh a certain mystique, knowing that Daddy would be so impressed to learn that I was going out with what he would call "an Aristocrat". Since Mummy's death when I was just twelve, I was the apple of his eye and he wanted the world for me.

'But I waited until my twenty first bonanza was over and then divulged the good news to him: I was engaged to Hugh; a peer of the realm. In fact, he was destined to be a City Banker and played down his title, but he promised that we would live in luxury as soon as we both graduated.

'You can imagine Daddy's reaction. He was thrilled to think I was entering a privileged and affluent world, but worried that I might feel out of my depth.

'As it turned out, he was right. Hugh had seemed so down to earth, so approachable when we were clubbing in downtown Manchester. But as soon as we arrived as newlyweds at his parents' huge country pad in Wiltshire, it was as if he entered another world . . . his world, and he reverted to his true self, leaving me feeling totally inadequate and trying to fit in to a lifestyle which was alien and daunting to me. I must have been mad not to have insisted on visiting his family prior to committing myself, but every time I suggested we visit them, he said it was best to wait until we were married. Apparently they did not approve of youngsters "living in sin" before tying the knot. Talk about archaic.

'Blimey! You mean you never even met his folks before you married the guy?' Diana sounded incredulous.

'I used to plead with him' Julia continued. 'At least tell me about your parents'. Hugh had painted an enticing picture of our future life split between London and the countryside. He would enthuse about shoots and dinner parties, hunting and household staff, as well as shopping in Knightsbridge and nightclubs in Mayfair. On hearing his stories it was little wonder that I lapped up the idea of living somewhere luxurious with the man of my dreams.

'Hugh always appeared to have a generous streak, but never seemed to have any money on him. "I don't do cash . . . like the Queen," was his explanation'.

Caz exploded with laughter. 'Really! You must be joking!'

'No, Caz, Julia replied, I'm not joking. I had told Hugh it was ridiculous, but he just smiled and said "It's the Pemberton way."

'"Where will we live?" I pestered him.

'Father will organise something for us. All in good time, my darling."

'He talked vaguely of grand houses in Belgravia, smart penthouses in Canary Wharf and country cottages in the Cotswolds where we could settle down and start a family. "At least four children, darling" he prophesied. Well, ok, laugh at me now. I deserve it. I was naïve and just wanted to believe him. At no time did he mention the huge influence of his parents, and worst of all the fact that we would be living with them under their jurisdiction.

'So, after our wedding in Chelsea Town Hall, just imagine my shock on arrival at his family's place in Wiltshire. Not a house, more a stately home inhabited by his parents, numerous staff . . . and now us. It soon became obvious I was expected to fit in and lead a life of boredom stuck out there in the country. All talk of Knightsbridge and Mayfair was forgotten. Hugh was up in London every day frantically busy on his trading floor, whilst I was stuck in the sodding countryside with no-one to talk to and nowhere to go. I couldn't even be a "lady who lunches," not a restaurant for miles and without Harvey Nicks, nowhere to shop. Oh yes, my father had got it right about being out of my depth, but in those early days I was full of hope that things would change.

'In any case, I loved Hugh, so I made an effort to adjust to married life. What a learning curve! I had to spend my days finding some sort of occupation until Hugh arrived home mid evening. By then dinner had been served by waiting staff to just me and his parents; they even had a gong to announce it, can you believe. So I had had to make small talk with them, aware that the staff were doubtless laughing at my efforts behind my back.

Of course, it wasn't really his parents' fault. They came from a different world and found it hard to understand why their precious son was choosing to make money at an investment bank in the City rather than learn the ropes of overseeing their family heritage. And I must have been a huge disappointment. I'm sure that their hopes had been for Hugh to marry a country-lass, hopefully from a family mentioned in Burke's Peerage, who would slot into the Pemberton lifestyle without difficulty and prove herself a worthy wife and lady of the manor.

'Sadly, Hugh seemed incapable of understanding my dilemma and declined to criticise his parents, or stand up for himself. He just made sure he was out of the door at crack of dawn and not back until late . . . if at all. He urged me to toe the party line, as he called it, and enjoy my life of leisure. Fat chance.

'"What's going on Hugh? I never see you now," I wailed, thinking of all the parties and pubs which we had enjoyed together in Manchester. But I soon realised, that was the Hugh of the past. He was now under his parents' roof and it seemed that his father controlled the purse strings. Where was Hugh's money going? I wondered. Did he have some other woman in London? I began to fantasise about a possible double life which Hugh was operating. But then I reasoned, working hours were notorious in the banking world, and he kept telling me he was making the most of his opportunities before he burned himself out. It was all to ensure a good life for us in the future – or so he said. And I tried, I really tried to believe him and to relax as instructed.

'For a while I settled down a bit, I suppose. The novelty was enough to keep me interested, and I enjoyed being "one up" on some of my friends in

Croydon who had settled for conventional marriages in the depths of suburbia. Their phone calls began to bore me with tales of their humdrum activities, and I could feel they were wary of asking about my new life. Contrary to me, they were always concerned about money. So I really was lucky, I kept telling myself . . . no money worries, a beautiful home and a successful husband. And, in the limited time that we were together, there was still a frisson . . . at least there was on my part. So did it matter that I had my degree in History of Art and yet no likelihood of putting it to good use? No, it was the University experience that was important, I consoled myself. Did it matter that I was bored to sobs and had lost my friends by moving out of their comfort zone? Absolutely not, I could try to make new, more appropriate friends here in the country. But most of all, did it matter that he was financing some sort of double life with another woman in the City. Maybe he had set her up in that Canary Wharf penthouse he had mentioned before we were married. I was beginning to drive myself mad with speculation, whilst at the same time yearning to be a model Good Wife.

'All right, I can see your eyes glazing over. You don't want to hear about the good times and how I tried to make my marriage work. You want me to cut to the chase. When did it all go horribly wrong? Well, after the birth of our gorgeous son, Edward, Hugh became more and more distant. In fact, I hardly saw him and, when I did, we had nothing much to say to each other. I felt that having produced the obligatory heir, I was of no more interest to him. Honestly, that's the sort of world his family inhabited.

'So I began to feel like a prisoner. Nanny took care of Edward and I was redundant. Relief came to me in the shape of a vodka bottle. It started innocently enough – just the odd one at lunch to get me through the day until official "sundowners" in the drawing room on the stroke of six. Then it became several glasses at noon, continuing through lunch and the afternoon, so there was no gap without. But when I began to reach for the bottle on waking, and lost my appetite, my memory and my dignity, I realised that I was well on my way to becoming an alcoholic . . . if not already there. There was no way I could carry on this routine, making excuses about avoiding Hugh's parents who must surely have drawn their own conclusions. Hugh stayed away more and more and I became incapable of maintaining any pretence that I was coping.

'But even though I knew it couldn't go on like that indefinitely, I was overtaken by a rapid turn of events. Without warning, Hugh pulled a fast one. One morning, over the first vodka bottle of the day, I found myself reading a summons: Hugh was suing me for divorce, citing my unreasonable behaviour due to alcoholism, and stating that I was incapable of caring for our son and even posed a danger to him. I could hardly take in all the legal terms as my mind was so raddled with drink. Don't ask me to explain; I've blocked out the sheer awfulness of what followed, but, looking back, I'm sure his father pulled strings with his impressive network of legal contacts in order to get me permanently out of their lives. Suffice it to say, our divorce was granted post haste. AND custody of Edward was granted to Hugh. I might eventually be allowed minimal access under close supervision . . . but only if I successfully relinquished my alcoholism and the authorities were convinced I posed no threat to my son.

There was a stunned silence around Julia.

'Well, it took over a year for me to get sober. Daddy was amazing; he organized my rehab care, paid for everything and asked no questions. And although he may have been thinking "I told you so", he never uttered the words. It must have been hell for him. I spent most of the year crying my heart out, leaving behind my child and my marriage and knowing I would have to face what Daddy called "a new chapter in my life".

'True to his word, he wasted no time. Once I was out of rehab, he contacted the authorities to start the process of gaining access to Edward. By then, Hugh was already hitched to the other wretched woman. Yes, I had been right about that side of things. So there was no chance of getting Hugh back. I was depressed, yet knew I had only myself to blame. How could I have failed so dramatically? How could I have let bloody vodka triumph over my husband and my son? There's no answer. And no second chances. But I would fight back for my son. What mother wouldn't? I discussed strategy with Daddy. "We've set the wheels in motion, but it might take a bit of time" he said wisely. "Meanwhile I'm sending you on a cruise to meet some new people". He really thought I could just start again. Well, for once, his kindness has misfired. What's he going to do to get me out of this ghastly lifeboat? I fear even his paternal power has no influence in the middle of the ocean.'

Chapter 15

It had been a bumpy ride but, as the day wore on, the sun returned to blaze down on the raft from an azure sky. Only the steep swell remained of the previous night's storm. There were few who had not told the company something of their lives. In the hope of defusing the animosity, she sensed building over the fiasco of the wasted chance of rescue; Jenni looked around for someone to continue the dialogue. Caroline Cavendish had been heroic in the first few hours of their adventure; perhaps she was the one to take their minds off their plight.

The Lawyer's Tale

'You want to know my story? Well, right at this minute there is only one story on my mind and that is my mother. I'm doing my best to rationalise this; to tell myself she is not missing.   I just don't know where she is. She may be on one of the lifeboats. Probably is. Just because I couldn't find her doesn't mean she didn't get off the ship. Oh God, I mustn't go there. Stay positive. She's most likely floating on a raft close-by somewhere. I guarantee she'll be driving her fellow-floaters insane by now, controlling them, taking charge. Only unfortunately, her logic has become a little skewed in recent years. I wouldn't be surprised if they all jump raft and take their chances with the sharks.'

'What happened, Caroline?' The Cruise Director recalled the mother and daughter from her passenger roster.

'It's 'Caz'. My friends call me Caz. I was finishing dinner. My mother had left the table. Insisted on going back to the cabin on her own. I should have gone with her, but how was I to know the ship would go down? She'd had wine on the top of her medication and felt a bit woozy. I really should have made sure she was all right, but, well, I suppose I just wanted some space to have a normal conversation for a bit. She isn't too well you see, hasn't been what you might call 'herself' since my esteemed father left her for his scheming little masseuse a few years ago.

'Oh dear, I shouldn't be telling you that. Must get my head together. All this will seem like a great adventure in a couple of day's time. We'll all be developing wonderful anecdotes to tell at dinner parties. How we considered having to eat one of our number for the rest of us to survive, but were rescued just in the nick of time by a bunch of hunky marines with thrusting thighs. Or how we bravely caught fish to eat and saved condensed water whilst we fought off a variety of monsters etc.'

'But what about your story Caz?' Jenni tried to coax the girl to focus on happier times. 'Come on, tell us about your life and who you are. It's what we're all doing. It'll help you get your head together, as you put it. Entertain us!'

'Well, I'm not sure anything I have to say will be very entertaining and as to "who I am," well, I can't tell you that since I don't know myself. That's why I came on this cruise: to try to find out.

'Look, I'll just start from that point. Booking the cruise. I've been living in Singapore for the last seven years. I work as a shipping lawyer and I moved there after doing a couple of years learning the ropes at Broadgate, central London, after qualifying. With Max, my boyfriend, who works for the same firm. We managed to get transferred together. It's all been great, but I suddenly began to question everything we were doing. The way we were living. What I felt about him. Ungrateful cow, I know. We had a fabulous life, living in a glossy condo with lots of glossy professional people just like us. It had all the facilities: floodlit pool, gym, tennis courts, tropical gardens etc, etc, right in the middle of Chinatown, a ten minute walk to the financial district where we worked in a state of the art, climate sensitive, award winning sky-scraper and earned a fortune. What was I thinking? Most people would think it was pretty damn good. Weekends chilling out on tropical islands, or partying with smart, beautiful people. We worked long hours too though. The firm got its money's worth out of us, but I was brought up to work hard and I've a good brain. It just started to occur to me that maybe I could do something a bit, well you know, more satisfying with it.'

'I think you are telling us here that maybe you felt sort of empty inside?' Julia leaned across the sleeping Franny to lend support.

'Well, that's a bit of a new-agey way of putting it, but I suppose I did. It all goes back to my mother really and what's happened to her. She spent her life doing the "right thing". She'd been the perfect corporate wife. Made a career of it. My brother and I

169

were both born in London; she organised that between living overseas with Dad, so that there wouldn't be any problems with our passports. Typical of how she controlled our lives. It began there. We had to be better than anyone else. Went to the best nursery schools and were learning French by three, along with the violin. Ouch. I dread to think of the noise we extracted. Anyway, you get the drift. Typical pushy, middle-class, mother. I've been jumping through hoops since I was born and one glorious evening, watching the clichéd sunset in Bali, I started to wonder who or what I might have been if I'd had a different life. Self-indulgent, I expect you're thinking, but Bali does have that sort of effect. There's something about the luminous beauty of the land, the dramatic seas and, despite the third-world poverty of the people, their grace and reverence for the life of spirit is very touching. So much for being a hard-nosed lawyer, helping to keep the flow of money spinning around the world through the same hands. I suddenly thought "what if the world didn't have to be run by giant corporations and self-seeking politicians? What if these people are right? That there is something more . . . better." I expect you're thinking that my mental decline is beginning earlier than my Mother's did. You may be right. But this idea kept eating at me. Max couldn't take it. A great believer in hedonism is Max, and poking the other guy in the eye before he gets you.

'So there we are. I got a strange idea and suddenly I wasn't satisfied anymore, so I left. Much to Max's relief I suspect. Got transferred back to London where I intended to work until I had mulled things over a bit. But then, something extraordinary happened which I see now has forced my life to change. I won the lottery. Not just a few million. One hundred and sixty-five million. So I bought two tickets for the cruise and here I am. The question is: will I ever get to spend it usefully or will I drown here knowing that I was a shallow, uncaring bitch. And where is my mother?'

Tony reached for her hand once more and held it tight. It was such a comfort to have this person pressing his skin to hers. She leaned in to rest against him and the empathy, that flowed between them suddenly, brought all the emotion of the past few hours to the surface. Caz sobbed and he squeezed her hand again. However, she was made of strong stuff. What was a little shipwreck to a girl who ate all her male colleagues for breakfast?

'Is that why you chose a cruise for your thinking?' Jenni said sitting opposite and stretching forward to listen to the quiet spoken woman. 'Because you're a shipping lawyer?'

'Maybe. Yes, I suppose I had the idea that, instead of sweating over one, I could recline in luxury on one instead. Huh. I'd have been better off on a ferry to the Isle of Wight. And so would Mum . . .'

'She'll be on one of the boats. Don't you fret.' Tony said in comforting tones.

'Everything I've done since I left Singapore has been weird. I mean, I don't even do the lottery normally. Most probably look down my nose at people who do. I know, I know...I come from a privileged background and it's easy to sneer. But we all know the odds.

'Why then? 'Tony asked.

'I met a couple of school-friends for lunch. We got completely wasted discussing my predicament, then we fell out of the bar and they made me buy a ticket. I mean, I'd never be poor. Daddy's not short, but he wasn't pleased with my decision to leave Singapore. Not about my boyfriend though. He was happy I'd dumped him. Said Max was a bit too pleased to be connected to our family.'

'Your father, I take it'll be Charles Cavendish of Cavendish International?'

'Oh, er yes, that's right. I'm sorry; I don't really like talking about my family.'

'I suppose once people know who you are, they're all over you, are they?'

'Something like that. It can be difficult to know when people are genuine.' Caz felt Tony flinch and begin to withdraw his arm. Caz pulled him back, closer. 'Please don't,' she whispered. 'Keep me safe.' 'Anyway,' she spoke louder now, to the group. 'I always wanted to make my own way, was brought up to. I think my mother's dream was for me to become Prime Minister. It would justify all the years she's spent training me to win.'

'I don't blame your dad loping off with a little masseuse.' Ken had perked up at the mention of the millions. Must've been hell for him, living with a woman like that.'

Caz sighed. 'Yes, I suppose you're right when I think about it. The perfect wife, with perfect hair, organising his social life to an inch of his life. Poor mum, she saw it as supporting him. She had files on people you know, which she kept up religiously.

Every scrap of information gave her power. Yes, I see it now. Of course the little masseuse doesn't do the social scene. Just drags Dad off on jaunts to the seaside with the kids. They've got a cottage in Norfolk. He rolls his trousers up and makes sand-castles on the beach.'

'There you are then. Lucky bloke,' Tony said, 'bet she's a cracker too, this stepmother.'

Caz laid her head on Tony's shoulder. In her family, their business was their own and she had said far too much. The water surged and sucked beneath them and Caz tried not to think of the depth of it beneath them and the miles and miles of it in every direction. Surely there must be massive searches going on. Maybe her mother was right at this moment being winched into a helicopter. It was odd that she didn't feel more frightened. Even though she had hardly spoken to this man who was imparting so much comfort, it was almost as if they didn't need to know anything about one another. Their bodies seemed to know all that was needed. She fell into an exhausted sleep.

Raft of Life

Chapter 16

Although the raft continued to rock and twist in the still turbulent sea, most of the passengers, with the aid of frequent doses of Cinnarizine, had acquired some semblance of sea legs. None exactly looked well but, thanks to the collection of overnight rain, they had been able to rinse some of the salt from their exposed faces. Chapped lips, dry skin and occasional lesions were apparent on all of them.

The Sparrow's Tale

The last story teller had just finished. Jenni noticed that the previously barely mobile Clarissa Sparrow had shuffled closer to take an interest in what the soft spoken Caz had been saying.

At length Clarissa spoke, 'I'm so sorry, I didn't mean to disturb you, but the stories are interesting and I wanted to hear more clearly.'

'Right, so now you know what the score is, how about you making a contribution instead of hiding away like a little mouse.' D.J. was getting less tolerant.

'You really want to know my story; yes I do need to get it off my chest, so here goes.' For once she sat up straight and addressed them all.

'My father, the Reverend Cyril Sparrow, married quite late in life to Daphne, who spent most of their married life as a semi invalid. They had no children of their own, so I was adopted from a home for unmarried mothers. I often felt, as a child, that my adoptive mother really only tolerated my presence because I was quite an attractive toddler with masses of wavy auburn hair and possessing unusually large eyes of a bright emerald green colour.

'I was also a quiet, reserved child, surprisingly docile, which most definitely suited my mother. When I started school, I never had many friends. Indeed it was quite the opposite, called stuck up for being the vicar's daughter, ridiculed for having a stupid name, Clarissa Sparrow, but mostly made fun of because of my hair. I was called, "ginger nut," or "carrot top," which I hated. However, I never gave them the satisfaction of knowing how much their taunts and jibes hurt, but I did manage to get my own back in a few small ways. Hiding their gym shoes just before games lesson or "accidentally" tripping them up in the playground. I knew these were rather low tricks but got quite a lot of satisfaction from my revenge.

'Later on, I heard whispered comments which also hurt my feelings. "What scary and unnerving eyes she has, like green glass boring into you. They really are quite frightening; she must be like a bad spirit or witch, better steer clear." I decided to put this down to their total ignorance and take no notice of them. However I did adopt the affectation of wearing tinted, heavy horn rimmed spectacles, so that my eyes were not so noticeable. Thus disguised, they gave me instant anonymity and privacy, which I relished, especially later on in life.

Julia sympathised, 'what nasty children; they shouldn't have teased you like that, but do go on.'

'A vicar's daughter must uphold the standards that his special position in society demands. This mantra was constantly drummed into me by my Aunt Dorothea. She had married a much older and very wealthy man who had died long before I had any recollection of him. But Aunt Dorothea was a different matter. She visited her brother about three or four times a year and we were all united in our dread of the visit. My mother coped with it by retiring full time to her bed, father to his study, apparently writing innumerable sermons, so it was left to me to take the brunt of her reorganising, attempting to change everything we held dear. She offered nonstop advice and expected it to be implemented immediately. She also felt it was her duty to teach me some acceptable society manners and outmoded etiquette. Aunt Dorothea had one stepson, Douglas, a real ne'er do well, drinker, gambler and recently sent down from university. He had money placed in trust for him, but not to be released until his thirtieth birthday, so in the meantime he sponged off Aunt Dorothea He was forcibly made to accompany her on one of her visits to us when I was about 16 years old. I had no experience of boys, he knew it, and so just for amusement he decided to make a play for me. At first I was a little scared, but it was not long before it became quite a useful learning experience. Some sort of self preservation instinct must have kicked in; I actually took great delight in putting this abominable young man firmly in his place. I pretended for a while to be flattered, and then apparently acquiescing to his, not very well planned, strategy to get this young girl into bed. I quite enjoyed the mild flirting and teasing, seeming to allow a little more progress at every foray, but I had plans also. One night, having made a tentative previous agreement, he knocked gently on my door at midnight. Putting on what I imagined was an inviting and seductive voice, I cooed softly, "do come in Douglas." He eagerly barged in, as I thought he would, not noticing the rope strung across the threshold. He tripped up and dislodged a whole pile of large pots and pans, collected earlier from the kitchen. He fell heavily, making a tremendous racket, and then let out a whole string of invective at the top of his voice. The rest of the household came running, even my mother, to find Douglas in just his under pants, while I sat innocently on my, bed fully clothed, and feigning tears of worry and fear.

Amid general muffled laughter, Ken said, 'What a despicable chap, I trust he got his just desserts.'

'Oh yes, just listen. Clarissa replied, 'Aunt Dorothea marched him off immediately and the next day they had left before most of us were up. Douglas, we heard, was shipped abroad to work in one of his late father's overseas offices. To my huge delight, Aunt Dorothea announced that it was one of the least desirable and rather remote; so Douglas truly had his comeuppance and I did not feel one iota of remorse, I learnt revenge was sweet.

'A couple of years later I was accepted as a student nurse at a large training hospital in London. My time at the hospital was one of the happiest in my life. I was accepted as a friend by my fellow students and I also thoroughly enjoyed the nursing training. After just one year as a fully qualified nurse, I met a young doctor, an intern, who for some reason sought out my company. Peter was a serious and dedicated young man so we suited each other admirably. Our friendship grew slowly but steadily and we were soon, what is known as, "an item." But fate intervened and my mother became more seriously indisposed, needing full time home nursing. She announced, with what I felt was rather selfish insistence, that she did not want strangers around her, especially as she had a daughter, a qualified nurse, who could care for her. My appeals to my father where to no avail. He could deny his wife nothing, even though I was being seriously considered for the post of ward sister. No, I must give up my career and come home like a good daughter.

'Aw, that's not fair, shame.' Franny responded.

'So began several years of waiting on her hand and foot and forever being at her beck and call. Aunt Dorothea still visited, and in an uncharacteristic moment of sharing confidences I told her, ashamed as I was, that I was beginning to dislike and even hate my mother.

'"You do know," she began, "that you are not her real daughter only adopted." I recollected that I had been told this, but that was years before, and it had not made much impression on me. Once I had asked about my birth mother, which seemed to embarrass both parents. They said that they could tell me no more, as it was not allowed for adoptive parents to know about the birth mother at that time.

'"What nonsense," retorted Aunt Dorothea, with ill disguised glee, "your father was offered a baby from that home for wayward girls. He attended there at intervals to offer spiritual guidance to the girls, not that it did much good, but he also christened some of the babies before they were adopted. The Matron, knowing how much he loved children and that Daphne was not able to oblige, offered him one of the poor little waifs – you! And your father did meet with your birth mother."

Apparently, the home no longer existed, but the matron was still alive and Aunt Dorothea scribbled down her name and address, should I wish to contact her.

'So did you ever contact her? Franny asked.

'Yes, I did, but all in good time.

'I received a long awaited letter from Peter about then, informing me that he had been offered a hospital position in Africa where he felt he could get more experience of tropical diseases. This was an area that both of us had often discussed, studied together and even attended many seminars. We learnt a great deal about native plant life that could either cure or kill, often without being detected. We both found the subject highly intriguing and fascinating. Peter was sure that I could also get a nursing position at the same hospital and suggested I made enquiries. I might well have done so but for several reasons. The most persuasive question that Peter could have put to me was never even touched on and, when I tried to explain my desire to go to Africa, both Aunt Dorothea and father were aghast. They met my reasons for wanting to go with twice as many reasons for not going, the main one being, who would care for mother as well as I could. It was true she was certainly declining in both physical and mental health and in the New Year she passed on.

'Mother's death came as a shock to father, even though she had spent most of her married life complaining that she was not long for this world. Aunt Dorothea was adamant that I should stay home and care for father. 'It is your bounden duty as his daughter, even more so since from, misjudged, kindness he took you on.' Aunt Dorothea knew how to hurt, but I was learning from her. Many of father's female parishioners were only too willing to sit with him, make tea and generally make a fuss of him. Well, it gave me some time for myself, a real luxury and I could use this time well. Over the years I had become obsessed with finding out more about my birth mother. Finding the address that Aunt had written down for me previously I now had the time and the will to use this information. The home was still there, now taken over by the local council. None of the original staff remained, however I was lucky enough to speak to a woman who remembered the Matron and she gave me her present address. I waited until my letter to Matron produced an answer. I had not specified much, just that I had past connections and wished to renew old ties. So, two weeks into my searches, I was off to spend the afternoon with Matron. I made some effort with my appearance so I did not hide my wayward auburn curls under my concealing hat and I even removed my tinted spectacles. I found the little bungalow easily and rang the doorbell. I could hear the shuffling of feet down the hallway and sounds of fumbling as Matron pulled back a series of bolts. Her reaction when she peered closely at me was one of surprised recognition. 'My goodness, she said, 'I know who you are; you're the image of your mother, no mistaking that hair and those so green eyes.'

'I spent a very profitable afternoon. Matron was pleased to have company and her memory was extremely good so I patiently listened to all her stories while we drank innumerable cups of tea and made inroads into a delicious, homemade Victoria sponge. At last I got the information I wanted. She remembered that my mother had a visitor whilst awaiting my birth, a neighbour of my actual grandparents. As no one else was likely to visit, she had decided to do so. Matron had kept some personal information. She went through her appointment diaries and finally found the neighbour's name and address. Some ten minutes later, after thanking her profusely, I left feeling highly confident that I might be able to contact my real mother.

'I set out several weeks later to another nearby town and knocked on the door of a small terraced house. In response to my third knocking a rather gruff female voice shouted, "Alright, alright keep your 'air on, I'm coming." At the mention of hair, I patted my accustomed cap checking for escaping curls, as I did not want to be recognised straight away. As soon as I asked after her former neighbours she ushered me into a small parlour and, when I mentioned their daughter, she launched into her tirade.

"They had a daughter, Susie, pretty little thing, but such tantrums. She was uncontrollable and, as she got older, they became quite frightened of her. She used to smash up the house, punch and hit them both if she did not get her own way. She took up with a bad crowd and was constantly in trouble with the police, then she got pregnant. No one, not even her, knew who the father was and her, now elderly, parents could not cope at all. I tried to help, once, even visited at the home where she was to have the baby, turned out to be a girl. We never got to see the baby because she was adopted by a good family. Just as well, I hate to think what her life would have been. Probably never even make it to school age. Then she came home, started her bad ways again and landed up in prison. Her parents were re-homed by the council and thankfully, she was never seen again."

'I pressed a five pound note into her hand; she grabbed it and plunged it into a pocket of her grubby apron. I beat a hasty retreat; not quite the loving mother I had been hoping to find.'

'So what happened next?' Franny asked.

'Father just could not cope and, soon after, he too died. I did not feel any real emotional loss, but found I was able to fake it quite well and got a lot of undeserved sympathy and help from the bulk of his congregation. The Bishop visited, ostensibly to offer his condolences but really to make sure I was ready to move from the vicarage and make way for the new incumbent and his family. Father had left me with practically nothing so then Aunt Dorothea offered me a home at her rather resplendent country house. We both knew that the offer was really to obtain a grateful, willing, skivvy and companion. She had no family now, except Douglas and me, and I was obviously the lesser of two evils. Douglas had his regular allowance from the trust fund and now had no need to butter the old girl up. I had no such financial backing so Aunt Dorothea had me just where she wanted me, or so she thought. The next few years were sheer purgatory and I was subjected, day and night, to a stream of complaints and grumbles and was constantly reviled for my clumsiness, incompetence and plain stupidity. I took it all with meekness. I had my big plan to complete so I played my part to perfection.'

'And what was this plan?' D.J. said, 'Come on we want to know the outcome of all of this.'

'I guess none of you here can even remember seeing me around during the cruise. I have perfected the art of non detection, merging always into the background. A timid, mouse like, creature, looking and acting inconspicuously, in most cases, instantly forgotten. But always, with a razor sharp brain, working on a big plan. Aunt Dorothea had to trust just me implicitly and gradually come to rely on me alone. I had to become indispensable to her. Her doctor already trusted me completely and would always confide in me on health matters. After all I was a trained nurse. The few servants she still had made sure they had little contact with the miserable old woman, so I had the final say in household affairs, including all the financial running of the house. Her solicitor often furnished me with up to date information on her now limited, but still lucrative, business affairs. A new will was finally made and, as chief executor, I knew that I was also the main beneficiary. From now on Aunt Dorothea's health declined rapidly and nothing helped, the doctor put it down to general ageing. I was always a truly caring nurse, making sure she took all her prescribed medicines and, more importantly, her favourite evening tipple, which only I prepared.

My professional behaviour was exemplary but, despite, or maybe because of, my diligence, Aunt

Dorothea finally passed on. The doctor had no hesitation in writing the cause of death on the certificate as a mild infarction caused by months of gradual decline. So I inherited the lot, just a year ago. I finally felt it safe to leave my luxurious fortress and decided to take this cruise where *I* would be cosseted and pampered at last. All those years studying tropical medicines had paid off. But, those inherited genes from my birth mother, I knew just what a terrible person she had been and at that time it had not worried me too much. But it must have had some influence on my own behaviour. My need for revenge, and pay back for all I had endured throughout my life, was very strong. However, the counter influence of my strict moral upbringing had left me with a largely unwanted conscience and a disturbing feeling that one should atone for one's sins. Try as I will, I cannot feel at ease or enjoy my comfortable situation. But I am not the down trodden, meek creature that you may think; I am not to be so lightly dismissed!'

At this point, she clambered awkwardly over the jumble of legs to the hatch. 'Now, if you will excuse me there is something I have to do.' She ducked out through the hatch and pulled the flap closed for privacy.

A buzz of speculation ran round the raft.' I didn't really believe all she told us was true, but what a way to live.'

'Whatever she did, you can't help feeling some pity for her, things could have been so different.'

'Did I understand that correctly,' Julia said to Ted, in hushed tones 'she just admitted to bumping the old girl off?'

'I don't know what to make of it,' Ted replied 'perhaps she was romancing.'

'Or is delusional,' Ken whispered.

'She's very quiet out there,' Franny was the first to show concern.

Gradually realisation dawned on the life boat occupants.

Jack Brownlow, who had been on lookout and had discreetly climbed back inside to give the woman some privacy called out, 'Are you alright, Clarissa?' There was no reply. 'Maybe one of you ladies better check up on her,' he said.

'I'll go,' Julia reluctantly pushed open the hatch flap and, seeing nothing, clambered out. 'Oh my God, she's jumped. 'Get the lifeline somebody, there's something in the water.

The passengers crowded the hatches; Tony stood up on the rim and hurled the quoit at an indistinct floating object. Knowing that Clarissa had gone, he slowly pulled the object in for Julia to reach down and grab. 'What is it?'

'It's that little hat she was so fond of!'

Chapter 17

As the officer in charge, it had been Jenni's idea for the assembled to tell stories from their lives. She knew that lifting morale, relieving boredom and finding reasons for them all to bond would boost their chances of survival. She had hoped that, in the telling, each would reveal a reason for the others to care about their continued existence and minimise any bubbling conflict.

Little had she realised then that revelations in her own story, when told, would be the source of some of the most serious quarrelling on board the craft.

The Cruise Director's Tale

Jenni had been dozing during a lull between monologues, and the candid and observant Ken saw two tiny tablets, slip from her now ripped skirt pocket. She had forgotten in the confusion that they were there and that she should have surreptitiously dumped them overboard. It was amazing that they hadn't disintegrated in the damp atmosphere inside the craft.

'Oh, so it's a case of do as I say and not what I do is it?' he boomed into the rubber and body odour tinged air. 'Typical of you bossy officer types. How come you didn't feel it necessary to swallow the tablets you forced down our throats then?'

'I have my reasons' Jenni responded, her mouth dry and her eyes full of salty sweat, accumulated as she slept. 'But I can't say right now, it's a personal matter'

'Not good enough, those damned things dry your mouth and make you drowsy. We all took them, why not you?'

'Ok, here it is, but to understand, you need to come back with me to my childhood.' She conceded, glancing at each reluctant and now awakened passenger individually. 'I may as well tell all of you my own story 'cause I don't think Ken is going to let this drop.'

Jenni made sure everyone was settled before swallowing hard. She readjusted her life vest, which squashed her, substantial and recently rather tender, breasts against her otherwise slim frame, and tucked her legs as demurely as possible beneath her. The gathering quietened down, and most suppressed the indignation they had felt when they first learned of her indiscretion.

'I was born to a well off, but not really wealthy, family in that no man's land between town and countryside, not quite suburbia,' she began. 'We travelled abroad quite a lot and I loved it. I had three big brothers, the oldest was a half-brother, and though I was teased unmercifully by them all, I suppose now that it made me strong. Mum often said she wanted a football team, but that I was the last, not because I was a girl but due to the curse of morning sickness.

'When the joshing really got bad, I always had my Auntie Claire. She lived alone in a bungalow converted from a barn at the bottom of our garden and, though she was only five years younger than Mum, she seemed so much more fun. Growing up, I thought that was because she was born in 1960, rather than in the 50s like Mum but, in reality, she had less responsibility, I suppose; I can see that now that I'm older. Due to her disability she couldn't work, and had never married, so her free time she devoted to me. It was my idyllic escape, and probably a relief for Mum too, to have one less child under her feet now and then '

'What's all this got to do with . . .' Ken interrupted

'I'll get to that in good time. It's not as if any of us has a pressing appointment, now is it?' Jenni frowned in the semi darkness.

'No, OK' conceded Ken, 'Carry on, but it had better be good; my tongue still feels like it has been rasped from those tablets, and yet I still feel dickey'

'Yes, you might feel it, but you can't actually be sick, and that's the point. Best for us all if no one barfs in the boat don't you think?' Jenni gave him a superior, quizzical look. 'Anyway, the biggest shock of my young life was when Auntie Claire died.' At that, a hush settled in the boat and Jenni had both their sympathy and attention.

'It wasn't that she had a short life expectancy, but that she had always been so independent. That meant she was driving one of those pale blue disabled cars, they used to have, on a foggy November evening. Do you remember them? I probably wouldn't have done if Claire hadn't driven one. They only had one seat and seemed to do just a couple of miles an hour. "Spakka cars," the kids at school called them, but I never saw Claire that way. She was just my auntie.'

'The Thundersley Invacars they were, fibreglass with a belt drive, worth a fortune, sold one at auction few years back' interjected D.J. 'They should have kept them rather than wasting good tax-payers money on huge Motability vehicles the scroungers can ferry their whole family around in at our expense.'

'Well that may be,' soothed Jenni, conscious of her job to pacify her audience, 'but politicking won't get my story told.

'Claire died in 1989 when I was just 11. It was bonfire night and she had never let not being able to walk stop her from doing pretty much anything she pleased. A local charity group she supported held a fund-raising bonfire and bar-b-q every year and she had been there as always on the front line, sitting in her wheel chair taking money as I remember. We left after the fireworks because it was a school night, but she had been one of the last to leave, and by then the air had been heavy with autumn fog, smoke and firework residue.

Her car was old, though it functioned well and met her needs. It may have been one of the last ones still on the road, but the shell, fibreglass as you said Mr Postlethwaite, offered her no protection from the potato wagon on its way to collect the next day's delivery. They say she died instantly and I hope that isn't just a platitude meted out to the grieving. She was too warm to have suffered any more than she already had done.

'Anyway, her death hit me hard. I couldn't concentrate at school, and my grades, never very good in the first place, began to suffer. Mum and Dad decided a holiday was the answer. They chose a cruise, Dad said it would, "blow away the cobwebs of grief" and, being early in the first months of the next year, I can't remember exactly when, we sailed to the Caribbean from Southampton.

'From the very first day on board I was hooked, I loved the sea, never felt sea sick, even around the Cape'

'Not a good enough reason to palm those pills, girl,' reproached Ken, wagging his finger.

'True, but hear me out. It's far more than that.

'I can remember now being dazzled by the importance of the crew, especially the ones dressed all in white with gold braid; even the size of the ship impressed me with its facilities. The ship was called Sovereign of the Seas and it seemed so exciting; totally different from package holidays and caravanning I was used to. We even had a balcony, an innovation on cruise liners back then. They had only just replaced the old windowed "Ocean View" cabins. I know now The Sovereign was only a couple of years old and the largest cruise ship at the time, but its grandness paled into insignificance compared with the life I imagined it offered.'

'Glad I had a balcony' interjected Isobel,' Would probably be still on there counting fishes if I hadn't jumped over, mind you, damned chair nearly came tumbling after me'

'Well', Jenni continued, after glancing sympathetically at Isobel, 'James, my next brother up and I attended the kid's club. They were in their infancy then aboard cruise ships. I think many of the passengers still expected children to been seen and not heard and were threatening to boycott, so the companies had begun to find ways of making us disappear. Marcus and Jerry, the older two were far too mature, in their eyes anyway, and had to content themselves with annoying the tutting classes by always winning at quoits and disrupting the games deck with their football.

'So that was where I met Sonia, a nursery nurse who had been employed to keep us entertained and out of trouble. Sonia became my idol and I fought to stay in the clubs, even on port days. They don't often let that happen now. The 'youthies' like their day off. I didn't see anything of St Vincent and had to be dragged on to dry land in Barbados. I have no idea what other ports of call there were, I simply wasn't interested. From that moment, I knew that a life at sea was for me.

'It seems funny now, but I was never very academic at school, stringing sentences together on paper was a nightmare, but I can remember being so driven that I spent weeks once we returned, composing letters to cruise companies and all my pocket money on envelopes and stamps. Most never replied of course, much too busy, and many would have been too hoity-toity to respond to a child, but a couple did. I'll bet they regretted it though, because I continued to bombard them with requests for information, and later, as I grew older, interviews.

'In the meantime, I tried to work hard at school. Even though I wouldn't need a university education, I did need to prove I wasn't a numpty. I also had an affinity with children and the disabled; Auntie Claire's legacy perhaps. So I worked at the subjects I felt I could pass, pretty much ignored the rest, and scraped enough grade 'C's to be accepted on the NNEB course at our local college. I still struggled though, especially with the written stuff, so it took me a year longer than planned, but it didn't really matter. I was playing a waiting game anyway. Cruise companies won't employ you until you are 21, no matter how many letters you have written to them.

'The college course finished when I was 19 and I filled the intervening years with child related jobs. First was an after school club, working for peanut shells. Peanuts are for the full timers, but on the whole, the experience did me good, and, through one of the mothers, I heard about a job at a special school. I didn't get the job, but they must have been a bit impressed because they kept me on file, and called on me now and then to fill in when staff were sick. I loved working with the kids; they remained so positive and happy despite their problems. Then, when the opportunity came to be a one-to-one carer at the school for Leanne, a physically handicapped 13 year old, I jumped at the chance. I wonder now, if I had been older when I was offered the job, whether I would have given up my cruise ship dreams. Leanne was incontinent and had seizures. It was hard work, but the atmosphere at the school was great. Had she not caught a bad cold in the October that I was 21, maybe I wouldn't be here now. She was a paraplegic, brain damaged through negligence at birth, which meant she could do little for herself, but oh, did she have a personality. She had a wicked sense of humour and, though she found it difficult to speak, due to her Cerebral Palsy, her intelligence was fine and she loved to joke with me. She became, in many ways, the sister

I never had, and the chance for me to repay my Auntie's patience and kindness.

The cold wasn't helped by her bus driver leaving her in the rain after school that Tuesday evening. He was in a rush and Leanne's Mum was stuck in traffic. He should have waited with her in the bus, but he broke the rules. We all do it now and again' she said pointedly looking at Ken.

'Her Mum was only a few minutes late but, by then, Leanne was sitting in a puddle in her wheelchair and she was shivering. The cold went to her chest and; with her low resistance and lack of muscle-control, she simply didn't have the strength to fight it. By the Saturday afternoon she was dead. Her Mum called me from the hospital, but I arrived too late to say good bye. Although I was paid for a month after she died, it was out of courtesy. My friend was gone and I had no regular job. I could probably have made enough doing supply at the school, I was known and trusted and staff absence is understandably high. I returned a few times but, without Leanne's wicked giggle, the place echoed with sadness. Around the same time, I realised my on/off relationship with Rick, a twice divorced DJ, with a son just a month younger than me, was going nowhere. So I did what I always did, wrote a begging letter to the cruise companies.

'This time, I had the benefit of age, qualifications and experience. I was called for an interview by Idyllic Cruise Lines and promised a letter to let me know within a week. I was cautiously confident as I drove my pink sprayed Peugeot, one of my Dad's indulgences, up the M40. It's a good job the cops weren't so hot on using mobiles back then, because, just as I sailed north of Oxford, I got a call to change my life. It was Justin, a man whose name I had found years before and to whom I had sent so many of those letters.'

'"Jenni", he said, "your persistence has paid off. You were right; you ARE just the person we need. Can you start next week, one of the youth crew on the Sunshine Village just quit and we need to fly someone to Majorca to meet the ship next Friday. Come back down here Monday and Tuesday for uniform and preliminary training. We can do the rest once you're on board."

'Could I just. It was the escape and new start I needed. I finished the journey with heady exuberance, not even minding the grinding traffic at the M5/M6 junction. Mum and Dad were delighted, and the brothers grunted. I spent a week shopping, saying good bye, driving and being trained. That journey is interminable you know. The A34 just goes on and on; totally monotonous, worse than this, well almost.

'The Sunshine Village was ICL's joust at the young market, not normally catered for on cruise ships. She was brightly painted, rocking with music and cheap to sail on. The clientele was, though. So most of the staid crew, who were used to the rich and snobby, said, "common as . . ." well you know what.

'I was assigned to the 'Perky Pirates' club for 5-8 year olds. I soon came to join my colleagues in calling them the Pesky Pirates and worse. If we were in the pool, they wanted the sandpit, if we were watching videos they wanted to be outside. Most of the parents dumped them with us from dawn till dusk and many were drunk when they eventually returned for them. All they ate was sweets, chips and ketchup, which made them hyper all afternoon.

'My favourite time was the night shift. All us youthies were on a rota to take care of the sleeping babies during dinner and the stage shows. That was my quiet time. I could watch a film, read a book and nibble chocolate from my stash. If a baby woke, all I had to do was page his Mum.

'We worked 10 hour days, 7 days a week, often in 2 or 4 hour segments with just enough time to grab some sleep in between. That is if your roomie wasn't rushing in and out or the neighbours didn't need the bathroom. We slept two to an inside cabin, with metal walls and bunks and the joys of a bathroom shared with next door. That's loads of fun if you forget to lock both the doors! The kid's clubs may seem colourfully dazzling and have their own deck but, outside there, we were restricted like third class on the Titanic. Goodness, sorry for that, very poor choice of words. We were, for the most part, below decks and invisible to the world with no interaction with passengers outside greeting parents, and little access to the sunny parts of the ship. Our only relief was the smoky ambience of the crew bar and the cheap drinks. We all got regularly plastered for almost nothing. When the crew club put on a party, for which we paid subs, all the wine and beer was free. We took great advantage of that, but risked our jobs. Being drunk meant having to walk straight and without swaying, carefully avoiding officers who could have you breathalysed, on the way back to your cabin. You have to stumble along Freeway, we called it M1 on British ships, from the crew bar to your cabin. If you are seen walking down, leaning on the wall, or swaying side to side there's trouble. The limit was two or three drinks, around the UK driving limit. More than that and it was pack your bags, off at the next port and pay for your own flight home. Definitely best not to be caught out in Porto Rico then, unless you fancied weeks roughing it whilst you persuaded someone to wire you the fare.

'Of course, we sometimes sneaked into the passengers' all night buffet restaurant, but I was only caught there once. I got carpeted for that and a verbal warning to boot. I was lucky, I could have been sacked. So I stayed as a youthie for four years, transferring from ship to ship, as per the company's whims, but saw a lot of the world. Well I saw a lot of ports, and the nearby chemists and supermarkets where I stocked up on headache tablets for the hangovers, deodorant for the parties and chocolate for the night shifts. I didn't see much of anything else, and that became a disappointment. I also got fed up with dodging security. After four years of being confined below decks, and no sober adult conversation, I had had enough. My childhood bedazzlement with the braided uniform renewed its call and I began trying for the entertainments department.

'Jobs are advertised on the crew notice boards and, as soon as a position came up, I applied for quite a few before my boss agreed I had the potential and recommended me for a job. I can't sing, can hardly dance, but he did feel that I was good at problem solving and relating to people. At last my cabin was promoted up a deck or two. Loads less stairs to climb. There are no lifts in crew quarters I'll have you all know, nor plush carpets. I still couldn't see outside, far too junior for an outside cabin, but no shared bathroom and, sometimes, no roommate.

'I soon learned the songs and actions for the sail away parties, though I sang quietly, and started to host deck quoits and quizzes. Those things I loved. Some of the really old passengers, and there are lots of them, are so grateful if you make sure they are near a speaker so that they can hear, or get a little help to stand whilst they throw their quoit. Interacting with people made me very happy. Then they asked me to speak on stage, with a microphone. My legs were jelly and, for the first time ever, I felt queasy with the ship's movement. I did take a pill that day. How I got through it I don't know; it must have been that the Captain, a tall, American, originally from Maine, who I was introducing, gave my hand a quick squeeze first. Wow, was that electric. He had seemed so remote before, but suddenly it felt like he cared. That was the start of a very exciting three cruises.

'I daren't tell you his name; he still works for the company, as does his wife who has a land job in Southampton since she had the kids. I'll just say my pet name for him was Bunny. Bunny was 40 to my 25, dark haired, well-built and very romantic. We tried to keep our relationship secret, screwing the Captain doesn't make you too popular with your colleagues, but he had a habit of stealing flowers from the displays and handing them to me whenever we passed in the corridors.

'After that first nerve wracking evening behind the mike, he asked me to join him for a night-cap in the officers' lounge. One stolen night became a ritual whenever he wasn't working the night shift. My confidence grew and, gradually I became more sure of myself, both on stage and off it, if you know what I mean?

'I wasn't under any illusions with Bunny. I was soon made aware by other girls in the crew that he slept with loads of girls, but always went back to his wife. I really thought I could handle it. Then, two weeks from home, on the third cruise, he told me his wife was joining him at the next port and that we had to put everything on hold. We slept in each other's arms that night, and I carefully cleared all trace of my presence from his cabin early next morning. Bunny slipped the cabin steward, an Indian lad who worked for half the UK minimum wage, a tenner to spring clean the cabin, and destroy any evidence of my existence.

'It wasn't until the third day of his wife's trip that I saw either of them. They were in the officer's mess, him in full crisp white uniform and her in a pale mauve floaty number. I walked in looking for a quiet meal after a hectic day, and she was there, straight ahead of me wiping gravy from a small boy's chin. Her hair was blonde and wavy, her smile bright and her eyes had a kind look to them. She stood when he did to greet me and I saw that the folds of the dress barely hid an advancing baby bump. I must have remained calm, but I know I was babbling about looking for some salad cream sachets. I left the room having shaken her hand and him from my life. Walking the corridor back to my lonely cabin, I vowed never to endanger another woman's happiness or family.

I still had plenty of fun, and quite a few liaisons, but I always did my best to ensure that they were not married or in a relationship. Life on a ship can be very incestuous, but I did not want to compromise myself again. A few of the relationships lasted a whole cruise, some a week or so, but most were one or two night stands and relief from the monotony. Then I met Gareth.

'We had both been with I.C.L for several years by then, and worked on the same ships a couple of times but didn't really know each other. When they launched 'The Star', they transferred their most experienced crew members to her. It was my first promotion as I joined her as ACD. Gareth, despite being with I.C.L for many more years, wasn't really interested in promotion, and was still working as an entertainments officer, leading sail-away parties and compereing quizzes.

'I wasn't really aware of Gareth, except that he was one of the more willing and obliging members of my team. He was always ready with helpful hints, and was the one person I could rely on to take on those tasks that everyone else avoided. He made me look good in the eyes of the Cruise Director and stopped me falling into the traps and pitfalls of a new position.

'Whilst I worked mainly daytime hours, helping to write the daily newspaper and organising the celebrity speakers, Gareth, more often than not, worked an early shift and then again at night in the theatre, introducing shows.'

'Celebrities? Who have you met then, anyone we know? The seemingly reclusive Franny asked.

'Yes a few over the years, Edwina Curry, the one who got eggs banned, Linda Thorson, you know, she was in Emmerdale as Rosemary King'

'More famous as being Tara King in The Avengers' murmured D.J.

'Yes, well, that must be before my time, I've only heard of the film, and she wasn't in that. Yes lots of others too, mainly comedians like Les Dennis. Most of them do their slots and stay in their cabins with room service, too self-important to mingle with the hoi polloi, but Edwina really mixed in. She was funny too, even though during her talk people only wanted to ask about her affair with John Major.

'Anyway . . . Diana, I first saw Gareth performing when he was introducing a mind reading act. For some reason they weren't ready, so he ad-libbed and started to sing. He has such a great voice. He can do Elvis and Roy Orbison really well but, on this night, in honour of the ship he sang her signature song, "Swing on a Star."'

A gasp came from Diana, at the other side of the darkened craft, followed by a cough and splutter, but Jenni carried on seemingly oblivious.

'I think I started to fall in love with him then. Soon it became obvious that we were sharing one cabin; mine because, with the promotion, I qualified for an outside one with a window rather than a porthole, and keeping all our stuff in his. Six months later, we were at a Take That concert on a two-night Barcelona stop over, when he went down on one knee and proposed. He had even bought a ring. White gold and amethyst, it's gone now. I left it in my jewellery box because my fingers have been so swollen the last couple of weeks.' A large tear welled up in her eye and slowly made its way down her cheek.

'We married on a beach in Fiji, with just my parents, his died years ago.'

'Is it Gareth who's on the radio every morning, the blond bloke that comperes the evening show? He always starts with that song you mentioned, "Swing on a Star". Franny was more animated now.

'Yes that's him. He took on extra work for more pay because we're saving to get away from the ships. We have a dream of setting up a dive shop, somewhere warm. Diving is our passion and one thing we have always had in common'. Jenni turned now and glared at Diana.

'You didn't know that did you? You scheming bitch'. I bet you had dreams of swanning off into the sunset with MY husband.'

'I . . . but, I only wanted to sing with him, I thought he had a telly offer and that it could be my big break, but . . .'

'Telly offer, what on earth made you think that?'

'I-I over h-heard it,' Diana stuttered. 'On the first day of the cruise, he was on the phone in your office and I was waiting outside to replace my laminex badge.'

'Good grief, you fool, it was "Jax the Max", the previous DJ, who got the offer, on some Top of the Pops type of show, a minor Sky channel are doing. Gareth was just agreeing terms to cover his work'

'Oh my God' gasped Diana. 'I thought he was giving me the come-on when I wrapped my legs around him on the opening song each night.'

'Wrong again, you Bimbo' spat Jenni. 'And what is that first song?'

'Swing on a st . . .' Diana's voice faded below the lap of the waves on the rubber hull.

Jenni's voice was harsher and more insistent. 'Yes, Swing on a Star; OUR song. He insisted he was to sing it each night as part of his agreement to work so many bloody hours.'

'But he looks straight at me when he sings the last verse. "You can be better than you are, you could be swinging' on a star."'

'No Di, he sings the words for me. He says, I will "be better off than you are", meaning away from that bloody overgrown bathtub, and the times when he looks at YOU are the first two lines, "And all the monkeys aren't in the zoo, every day you meet quite a few," but my preference for a song to you would be "Jolene."'

Ken lunged forward to stop Diana taking a swipe at Jenni. 'I think you had better not do that if I've been reading this story right, Jenni. You have a good reason for not taking those tablets, don't you?'

'Yes, and it doesn't seem right to share it with you all. You see, I don't know where Gareth is, or even if he is safe. We always vowed we wouldn't leave the ship apart; that we would find each other and leave together, even if it cost us our jobs. Now I'm here and I have no idea where he is' Jenni dissolved into sobs and Julia moved forward to hug her tight.

'Calm down now Jenni, you have more than yourself and Gareth to worry about now, I think,' soothed Julia 'Tell everyone why you didn't take those pills.'

Raft of Life

'Ok, Ok' Jenni resumed her story with a snuffle. 'I told you about my Auntie Claire and her being disabled. Well she had no legs and one of her arms was really short. You see, like my Mum, Nanny Edna was plagued with morning sickness, and when she was having Claire, she took Thalidomide; with disastrous results. Now I'm pregnant. Gareth doesn't know, he's always doing the radio show when I throw up in the morning, so that's why I simply couldn't bring myself to take the tablets. We only got separated because I'd nipped back to the cabin to do a test. The blue line appeared just as the ship shuddered and we heard the explosion.'

'Oh God, Jenni', pleaded Diana, 'I've been so stupid; I'm sure Gareth is fine. If only Franny's phone worked you could call him. He gave me his number; it's here in my pocket.'

Chapter 18

As the sun went down on the third day of their confinement Jenni looked speculatively at the last of her charges. He'd been resistant to every effort she made to involve him in the conversations. He responded with single word answers to practical enquiries such as did he want something to eat or drink and so on and had stood his turn on watch in stoic silence. He was either the most traumatised of the group or had some deep dark secret that he was determined to hide.

The Convict's Tale

Under Jenni's intense scrutiny, the man stirred from his sullen pose on the floor of the raft, 'Yeah, I know. I've been sitting here, listening to all you ladies and gentlemen telling your stories about how you've got into this – how'd you call it? – predicament, situation, or whatever, and kind of dreading when you'd get around to me.

'I still don't know whether I should say anything or not. You see, I'm not your kind of person. Not, what you might call, of the same class or whatever. If class means anything. After all, you get all sorts of folk in the world these days, pretending to be what they've really got no rights to. Not that I'm saying that any of you aren't out of the top drawer, or that. But you see these cruises advertised all over the place, and they're not restricted to those who've made their pile honestly.

'Don't misunderstand what I'm saying. I don't want to offend anybody. I'm the last person in the world to point the finger at others. All I'm trying to say is that, in the old days, you used to know who were the toffs . . . the real gentlemen and their ladies, like folk used to say. And you knew who the others were. The jumped-up ones, and the what d'you call 'ems . . . the nouveau riches? But these days, you just can't tell.

'Not on the outside, that is.

'Inside's a different matter. But you can't see inside. Not unless you're a bleedin' psychiatrist or something. No, it's only yourself what can see inside. To see the things that you're ashamed of, the things that make you cry out in the dark, the things that make you hope that there isn't a God after all, or else He'd find it so hard to forgive, despite all the things that the preachers say about Him.

'I know. I've been there. I've lain curled up at nights with an ache in my soul. If I've got a soul, that is. Who knows? Layin' there, waiting for the light in the morning, and knowing that it would be as dark inside as during the night. Days and days, week-in and week-out, months and years, and counting all the time. Counting until the time would come when you'd be free of it all, the persecution, the petty having-one-up, the sweat and the extinction of dignity.

'I'm sorry, I'm rambling.'

'It's about time you said something. You haven't joined in any of the conversations or anything,' Ken admonished the man. 'I can't even remember your name.'

'Have I not told you my name yet? It's Jack, Jack Brownlow, although I have had some other names during the course of my different careers. But you can just call me Jack.

'Well, Jack Brownlow, everyone here has told their story except you, Get on with it, man.' Ken's raised voice drew the attention of almost everyone on the raft.

'You really want me to tell my story, do you? Well . . . here goes, although I warn you, it might not be as pretty as some of you might like.

'To start with, it's only a chance that I was on that ship at all. I'd just happened to see it advertised as I passed the travel agent's window, that day last January, shortly after I'd come out. I'd found somewhere to live – only just more than a squat, it was – and I used to go along the street and into the main road, just to get a glimpse of other human beings sometimes. That's what being locked away leads you to, you know. Have you ever been to the zoo early in the morning and watched what happens when they open the monkey cages, after the night? It's just the same there, you know. The monkeys just peer out to start with, as if they couldn't believe that there was some daylight and freedom again. They can't trust themselves to come out to start with as if it might all disappear all of a sudden. And then one or two of the bravest will venture, you know and then, all of a sudden, they're all there, chattering and jabbering away without a care in the world.

'It's just like that when you come out. You can't believe that there are people out there . . . people and streets, and buses and cars, all carrying on with the business of living, just like they used to before you went inside. Except that it's all a bit different now. After all those years, the buses and cars look different; the adverts in the shops are about different things; the people you hear on the streets are dressed differently, and they talk about different things.

'Thing I noticed most about the people was how many of them seemed to be stuck all over with all sorts of ironware and things, even in places that looked bloody painful. It looked as if there had been some sort of fashion going on which they all had to conform to. Queer to me, though . . . it almost made me feel sick to look at some on them. In another land completely, not the London I used to know.

'Almost as if you've been dropped into a foreign country. And you feel kind of shy to go and try to take part in it all.

'But I just happened to see this notice in a travel agency window, with the name of a ship and the words 'to Bermuda'. And that rang a bell. 'Cause that was where she'd said she was going, all those years before. Before the court case, before the sentence, before all those years and months . . . I've said that before . . . I'm sorry.

'So I went in and booked a cabin. The cheapest, below the waterline cabin, which was all I could afford from the scant sum they'd given me 'to get me started again', plus the little bit I'd had left over in the bank from those days before.

'And I kept myself to myself, almost as if I were a stowaway. I'd walk the decks at night-time, after all the jolly dance-music had stopped, all the bingo-games had finished, and you'd all gone to bed. I used to get a few left-overs from the kitchens, when the Filipino staff were clearing away the wasteful meals they'd prepared, and I would stand at the rail of the ship in the dark watching the stars and the waves until the sky started to get light again.

'And dream of the day when we would get to Bermuda, and I would be able to go ashore and try to find her.

'But then came the accident. Half-past seven in the evening, it was. I'd been lying on my bunk most of the day, drowsing. You get used to living the wrong way round, so to speak, and it's easy to do when you've got accustomed to living inside. So I was only just half awake when I heard that bloody siren sound off like the crack of doom.

'Couldn't make out what it was at first. Of course, I hadn't had the sort of benefit of the emergency drill all the rest of you'd had. But there were all these sounds of panic outside my cabin. All the Filipino waiters, kitchen staff and the rest of 'em. Banging, shrieking and running up and down the corridor, they were, till I thought I'd better stick my head out and see what the problem seemed to be.

'Bloody chaos it was out there as well. Couldn't make head nor tail of it for a moment or two. But then I grabbed hold of one of the Filipinos and tried to get him to tell me what was going on. I couldn't get any sense out of him neither, until I took him by the scruff of his neck and banged his head against the wall a few times to make him speak properly.

'"Ship sinking!" he cried out.

'Hell! That wasn't anything I'd even considered when making my plans to follow that bitch. But I wasn't going to finish up as a casualty myself. I wasn't going to stay down there below the waterline, and get myself drowned. Not after all those years waiting. So I dropped the Filipino on the floor and started off in what I knew was the direction of the nearest stairway up. It felt odd, though, and it took me a minute to realise that it was sloping downwards. But then I couldn't think of another way out in the opposite direction, so I staggered to the stair door and pulled it open.

'Bloody water poured in, almost a foot deep. And I'm not ashamed to say that I pushed and shoved with the best of the Filipinos and the rest to get out of that potential rat-trap. Might have pushed some of them under the rising water . . . couldn't say, but in those situations it's everyone for himself, I always say. And I found myself on the deck with the rest of you just as she was going to heel over. So I jumped, like most of you lot did. Even though I can't swim.

'And then I found myself being lugged aboard this . . . what d'you call it? . . . life raft? I don't know who did that, just found myself lying on the floor, vomiting up saltwater. So I've shied away from you all. Just lying against the side of this thing and avoiding your glances. But it looks as if my luck has run out this time.'

'We're all waiting,' Ken goaded impatiently.

'All right . . . I'll tell you the whole story . . . here goes.

'I suppose it all started about twenty-five years ago. Yes, that must have been when it was. I'd grown up in what was then a fairly tough part of London,

Hoxton. Before the days when it became a fashionable place to live and to travel to the City every day.

'Gentrification, they call it. Bloody toffee-nosed prats, I call 'em. No, in those days it was tough. Not unknown for there to be razor fights outside every pub at closing times, and the cops'd only go around in cars with three or four aboard – none of your suicidal foot-patrols in those days. Not on your bleedin' Nellie.

'I'd come from a tough family. My old man never actually did a stretch for anything, although he was *called in* once or twice by the local station for questioning. Always seemed to have a good excuse for being somewhere else, though. I wish I'd been able to inherit that particular bit of cleverness from him, but he would never let on as to his methods. "Keep 'em guessing, boy," he'd say to me, at the times he'd caught me with something that didn't belong to me by rights; a bike, or a radio, or something like that. "Where'd you get that from," he'd ask, giving me a clip round the ear. "Nicked it, eh? Bloody useless git," with another thump. "Take after your stupid mother, you do." And another imprecation in the direction of my poor defenceless mother, who did her best to comfort me after father had had his say and gone off towards the nearest boozer.

'Poor Mother! She tried her best to stop me from going to the bad and, while she was still alive, she made a pretty fair fist of doing just that. Saw me through a proper schooling and everything. She wasn't going to let me skimp on anything that way, even though I was tempted to skive off many days. The report that I, got at the end of schooldays, was a pretty fair result. Could even have gone to University if I'd been bothered. But then Mother sickened and died . . . can't say what it was could have been one of those galloping consumption things or whatever they called them in those days.

'I remember my old man and I going to the graveyard when Mother was buried. Dad swore at the Parson "What do you mean by all this praying and codswallop?" he shouted. But then he broke down and cried. I'd never seen Dad cry before, and it sort of shook me. He actually knelt down in the damp earth they'd dug out, and cried. "Forgive me, Elsie," he said. "I've been a lousy husband to you." And they had to actually pull him away when they started shovelling the earth back in the grave.

'But I found I couldn't get any reaction at all from all this. Perhaps because I'd recently got this girl and fancied myself in love. Even when Mother's coffin was being buried in soil, all I could think of was the next time that Flo and I would be together. And I'd be on top of her, and thrusting away like glory until she . . .

Ted interrupted before things got too graphic, saying 'Hey, there are ladies present.'

'Sorry, I'd got carried away. But I'm sure that ladies or not, you all understand perfectly well what I mean. After all, we've all done it, haven't we? Or are there any virgins around these days? No, virgins are as rare as hens' teeth.

'But Dad had got hold of me with a grip like a vice and we stood together as the coffin went down, and he more or less forced me to take some soil and throw it alongside his. But it made me feel more like vomiting than crying. And then everything seemed to

212

get mixed up inside me. There were pictures in my head of the worms and bugs eating up what was left of my dear mother, all sort of confused with me inside Flo, and I couldn't tell one from the other. And then everything went all black and red together and I found myself on the grass to one side of the grave.

'Someone was saying, "Give the poor lad some air, it's been too much for him," and then someone else came along with a glass of water. And, between them all, they managed to get me into a sort of chair, and they half-pulled me and half-carried me to one of the cars waiting at the gate and took me home. And all the relations were there, looking as miserable as sin, waiting to see what Dad was going to do. In the end he said, "Get out of here, all you lot. Can't you see that I just want to be alone here?" and he more or less threw the lot of them out.

'After a bit he poured himself another drink, and said to me, "You can do what you want, boy. You're old enough to decide for yourself. As for me, I'm going to Canada." Would you believe, he went upstairs then and there and packed himself a rucksack and a couple of old hold-alls, threw his black clothes on the bed and got dressed in a rough pair of jeans and a sweat-shirt, with sneakers, held out his hand for me to shake, and said, "Take care of yourself," and went out of the door.

'And I haven't seen or heard of him from that day since.

'But I moved in with Flo. She was in some sort of squat with a few other folks, and we managed to fit it comfortably enough. Then, after a month or two of course, she told me she was pregnant. I was sort of flabbergasted at first – never sort of connected screwing with the end result of a baby before – always thought it was the sort of thing that happened to other folk but couldn't happen to Flo and me.

'But Flo was as pleased as Punch. She was quite big with the baby and seemed to be proud of the way her belly stuck out like that. The other folk in the squat were pleased as well. They'd do all sorts of things for her to make sure that the baby was made welcome when it eventually arrived, and I sort of was included in the welcoming feeling. And I was able to get a few things, half-inching them, or "borrowing" them, to make life more comfortable like . . . a pusher, a cot, and some more expensive items as well, especially for Flo.

'So things were going along well when that dreadful day arrived. The day that eventually saw me end up here, where I am now, here on the floor of a floating tent in the middle of the Atlantic.

'We'd gone down to the Portobello Road Market to have a look at some baby clothes. There was a fair crowd of people that morning and folks were everywhere. All over the pavements and in the roadways, where barrows and stalls were set out. There wasn't really enough room for cars to get by, in any case they shouldn't be allowed to drive along there on market days. Some folk take no notice, though.

'Flo and I were standing at one of the stalls, looking over some things. I'd managed to get hold of a wallet, which was hanging out of some geezer's pocket, waiting to be taken. I had a look inside and could see that there was a fair amount of cash. "Get whatever you want, love," I said to Flo, "I've got the money for it." She gave me a sort of grin and bent over the pile of clothes and stuff there.

"Just at that moment along came a silver BMW from behind us on the street. Not driving too carefully, either. People were having to jump out of the way. I could hear folk shouting out, "Watch out for that crazy bitch." and turned round to see it heading straight for us. Then it side-swiped one of the barrows, and lurched out into the middle of the roadway again. I could see it heading for Flo and me, and I did what I could to try and shield us from being hit. But the driver must have hit the wrong pedal or something, because it came straight at us. I felt myself thrown onto the bonnet, and slide off to one side.

'But there was this awful scream. The bloody car hit Flo full on, and threw her across the nearest barrow where she fell, sort of crumpled up. I managed to stagger to my feet and get myself across to try and help her, but she was lying too crooked. She wasn't moving either, and there was a great pool of blood spreading from where her head had hit the iron rim of the barrow. The whole scene was sort of frozen onto my brain. I could see, as clearly as possible, the number of the BMW and the look of the woman who was driving it.

'Then I sort of fell over again, and the world went round and became confused and black. After what must have been some time, I remember I came to on some sort of stretcher. There was a medico of some kind beside me. "Where's my Flo?" I screamed at him, but he didn't reply, just leaned over and gave me some sort of shot in the arm. But then it was a long

215

time I must have been under. When I eventually came to understand what had happened, I was in a hospital bed. Some person came along and tried to explain kindly that Flo had been killed outright. The wheel had cracked her skull and she had also suffered internal injuries. And the baby was lost as well.

'It took me a hell of a long time to get over this, you can believe me. To put it bluntly, I reckon I sort of went out of my mind for a while. The other folks at the squat were very sympathetic and most of them tried to help me, but I found that the best help came from the drags of marijuana I got from some of them who were conformed druggies, and I'd lie there on the bed we used to share, crying and seeing Flo all over and over again.

'And always in the front of my mind was the number plate of that damned BMW, and the face of the woman who'd been driving it.

'In the end, and it must have been about four or five months later, I came to the realisation that the drugs were doing me one hell of a lot of no use. So I quit – just like that, cold turkey, and spent a couple of weeks sweating and getting back to normal thinking. Then I made a phone call, to an old acquaintance I'd known in the local fuzz. There's always one or two cops who are bent to a greater or lesser degree, and this particular guy owed me for something that's happened a couple of years ago.

'"Mike," I said to him, "there's a car registration I want you to get hold of for me, just quietly like. I don't want to stir up any unnecessary frights at the moment." He was back on the phone within a couple of hours. Gave me a name, and an address to go with it. Posh part of the world it was too, just off Avenue Road, up the back end of the London Zoo. I 'borrowed' a Jaguar I saw in a quiet part of Bermondsey one evening. I'd always got a spare set of skeleton keys with me in case anything happened to come my way, and the next morning I drove up Avenue Road, and parked, everything quite legal, a few yards from the house. The silver BMW was parked in the driveway. There was a speakerphone on the locked wrought-iron gates up to the front door, so I pressed the buzzer and waited.

'After a couple of minutes a voice said "Yes?"

'"BMW agents here," I said. "Can I speak to the owner, please? We've had some reports of faulty brake systems on the particular model here, and want to make sure that your vehicle is not going to be dangerous."

'"Wait," said the voice. After a moment, the door clicked open and I walked up to the front door. It opened as I approached and a sort of butler guy appeared. "Wait here," he said, "and Madam will see you in a moment or two."

'Sure enough, after a minute the blonde woman appeared. "What's this about my car being dangerous?" she said.

'I went through my tale again. "Do you think it would be possible just to have a short test drive around the street here?" I asked. "I could tell then whether we need to take it in to have any modifications made." She stared, then went back inside the house, to reappear a moment later with her handbag, from which she extracted a bunch of keys. I saw that the car-keys and those of the house were all on the same ring.

""'I suppose you'd better drive it," she said, "so that you can tell better than I could." She handed the keys over, and walked round to the other side of the car. I unlocked it and slid into the driver's seat. She fetched a remote control gadget from her handbag and pointed it in the direction of the driveway gates, which slid open. I started the car, put it into reverse, and backed out. There's not much traffic on the streets in that part of town, and it was easy enough to drive a few blocks away from where she might be recognised. I stopped the car under one of the big old trees lining that particular road.

""'Well?" she said.

""'Not quite sure," I said. 'Have you had any trouble with this in the past few months?'

""'No." But the look on her face told me that she was lying.

""'Strange," I said. "We had a report of this particular car being involved in a very bad accident in which a young mother was killed and another person rendered unconscious, due to apparent brake failure."

""'Who are you?" she said. "You're not from the BMW agents, I'm sure. And you're not from the police. I told them everything about that accident, and I was exonerated from any blame. They said the other people walked in front of me, which was true."

""'Was it?" I said. "Or were the police lying? To get you off the hook?" She had gone very white. "Let me tell you the real truth. No, don't try to get out of the car. I can easily lock us both in, and no one will ever see us. I am the guy who was knocked

218

unconscious. And the girl who was killed was my girl-friend, with the baby we were both looking forward to. Just because you were driving too fast, too carelessly, and without a damn care in the world apart from your self-centredness. Now, just you listen to me. You are going to get on the phone from this mobile here," and I handed her my own mobile, "and tell your butler, or whoever he is, that you are going to drive with me to the BMW garage and wait to have the brakes remedied."

'The fact that I had a knife in my hand, toying with it carelessly sort of, might have had something to do with the fact that she did exactly as I said. She must have been a damn good actress, though, because her voice didn't waver or anything like that, and I could tell that the butler fellow must have been satisfied.

'I started up the car and drove out of London, out into the lanes of that odd sort of bit of country between Essex and Hertfordshire, and parked beside the entrance to a field. "Get out," I said. "Out and over the fence into the field. Now, if anybody does just happen to come along, they'll think we're just a couple having a snog in the hay or something."

'Her eyes widened and I thought she was going to scream or something. "Don't worry," I said. "I wouldn't dream of touching you . . . you're not my type for that sort of thing. Now, be a good girl and sit down there, and we're going to have a good talk, you and I."

'I told her just exactly what it felt like to have someone you loved crushed like a rotten egg due to someone else's carelessness. I didn't do anything to ease her feelings either. All the hate and bitterness I'd had for the last months came right out and I let it pour over her. I'm afraid I called her every bad name I could think of, and a few more I'd forgotten I knew. In the end she was crying and shaking like a jelly. "What can I do to put things right for you?" she said.

'"The only thing that you've got, that I'd take, is money," I said. "Nothing else. And that, you must have plenty of, otherwise you wouldn't be living in Avenue Road with a butler and driving this sort of car. So, where are you going to get the money for me, and when? I reckon you'd better get it quickish, or else I might run out of patience."

'She sat there for a few minutes, sort of thinking. If I'd known then what I knew afterwards, I'd never have let her think so long. But then, always wiser after the event, they say. In the end she said, "Drive us back to Avenue Road. The butler is only a temporary day-time employee, in any case. My husband is in France on a business meeting. So if you wait in the car until the evening, I will let you in when the butler has left, and we can open my safe. I'll let you have what I can afford from there – it would be quicker, and with fewer problems, than if I go to my bank and ask for cash or a transfer."

"I thought it over. As far as I could see there weren't any snags, so I said, "OK, get up, and we'll go back in the car."

'I waited in that BMW until nearly ten o'clock, hidden for the most part under one of those big tartan travelling rugs posh people carry. I saw the butler guy come out of the front door, go across to the garage and come back with a bicycle. He opened the gates, must have had a remote control of his own, and disappeared up towards Swiss Cottage station. To make sure, I waited another ten minutes, then went across, and rang the door-bell. The woman opened it almost immediately; she must have been waiting in the entrance hall. "Come through," she said. "Upstairs . . . the safe is in my dressing room."

'Seemed quite logical to me, so I followed up the sweeping circular staircase and into a very plush room, all white and gold, with ivory-coloured furniture. Everything as swish as you could imagine. The woman was dressed to match . . . she'd changed clothes since the afternoon and was wearing a negligee sort of thing with a long train and the rest of it. "Would you like a drink?" she asked, opening a cabinet sort of thing and revealing as many bottles as you see in the average pub.

'I shook my head. "Just what I came for," I said. She walked across to a table, and opened a panel in the wall by the side. Behind there was a large-ish built in safe.

'"Turn your back," she said. But I've been in the game long enough to be able to hear the clicks of the tumblers without having seen them, and could have told you the combination easily by the time she'd finished. When I turned back she had a cash-box on the table and the door was closed again. "Here we are," she said, and unlocked the cash-box. Inside were a few undistinguished pieces of jewellery, and a bundle of notes. "Count them," she said.

'There was fifteen thousand pounds there in mixed values, mostly large notes. "And the rest?" I said.

'"There's no more," she said.

'"Liar!" and I backhanded her across the mouth. She was knocked to the floor and just lay there, looking scared. I took the key and opened the door in the wall. It was child's play to open the safe again. Inside were bundles and bundles of notes. A quick glance told me that there was about half a million there. "This is more like it," I said, and stuffed them all in a plastic bag I'd been carrying in my pocket.

'"Please, no," she cried. "It's all I have in England. I've got more in Bermuda. I've got property there, but there is no more here at all."'

'"Tough luck."

'"In that case . . ." and before I knew what was happening she had pulled a whistle from somewhere inside that negligee and given an almighty blast, and the room was suddenly full of cops. I couldn't do a bloody thing . . . I'd been taken for the biggest sucker this side of hell.

'What's more to say? She turned out to be the mistress of one of the top men at Scotland Yard, so what chance had a poor black guy like me got? At the trial the woman, and the cops, perjured themselves to buggery, telling the court that I'd attempted to rape her, that I'd used violence to get the money, and persuading the jury that I was the worst kind of black criminal they could ever expect to meet. And the sanctimonious old judge leered down on me as he sent me down for twenty years. He asked me if I had anything to say. Nothing, except to vow to myself that I would track her down one day, even if it meant going to the Bermuda to find her.

'The rest you already know. So what's the use of going on? Just to hope that one day I come up against her again. I've paid my penalty; she still has to pay hers.

Raft of Life

Chapter 19

The survivors were all feeling the effects of their confinement in the cramped and unstable raft. Exposed skin was beginning to peel from the effects of salt water and sun during the day. They shivered away the nights, although the temperature never fell below a balmy 17 degrees. Most had sores developing where their clothes rubbed which alternately itched or stung, making both lying still and moving about uncomfortable. The revelations of Jack Brownlow's story left them all lost for words. Exhaustion was the only incentive for sleep, with the prospect of another day like the last nothing to look forward to.

All Ashore

Ted sat on the edge of the raft, an arm carefully wrapped in a grab rope in case he nodded off and followed Clarissa into her watery grave. The hint of colour at the edge of the, up to then, indefinable horizon indicated which way was west. He watched as the glow spread upwards, obliterating the spectacular starscape that had been his only light source for the last two hours. He thought he could hear a low drone between the slaps of wavelets on their rubber bed but, when he tried to focus on the sound, it disappeared. He turned his head, scanning the horizon, hoping his ears would act like radar antennas and pick up the sound. He put it down to wishful thinking and, hugging his safety line, closed his aching eyes for a minute or two.

There it was again. Or had he dreamed it? The sun had risen enough to show one edge of its blinding orb, the sky was a graduated blend of gold to blue, with only the pole star bright enough to remain visible. Heart pounding he scanned for any sign of an aircraft. He wanted to waken all his comrades but as the sound continued to wax and wane he dreaded seeing their disappointment if it turned out to be a false alarm.

Ted peered into the raft's dark interior, only one of the shapeless lumps under their foil blankets showed signs of life.

'Tony,' he called in a whispered shout that was further coarsened by his dry throat.

'Alright, Ted, I'm just coming,' murmured McBride, as he appeared at the hatch clutching two containers of water. 'Here.' He handed one over.

'Sh, listen.'

Tony froze for a few seconds. 'What?'

'Can't you hear it?'

McBride eased himself out fully to stand on the edge of the float. Clinging to the roof of the raft he slowly turned his head this way and that. At last he said, 'Engines . . . That way I think.' He pointed to the northwest. 'Pass the glasses.'

Ted already had the binoculars trained in that direction but, seeing nothing, he deferred to Tony's younger and fresher eyes. Unhooking the lanyard from around his neck, he handed them over.

It seemed like hours before Tony said, 'Got it. Flying boat heading this way. Tell Jenni to get some flares ready.

Trembling with excitement and trepidation, Ted clambered inside and found the sleeping cruise director and prodded her awake.

She jerked upright at his touch, looking wildly around. 'What . . . Sorry, bad dream,' she croaked, a confused look on her face. 'Ted?'

'Outside, 'Ted whispered, still reluctant to disturb the others. 'Bring the flares.' But the others were stirring already some were asking what was going on.

Jenni tried to raise her voice but started to cough uncontrollably. That got everyone's attention. Clearing her throat, she managed to say loudly, 'Nobody move.' Thinking, *this is a stick up,* to end the phrase. She smiled and said, 'We can't afford any mistakes this time.' Clambering over several squirming bodies she retrieved the pack of flares from their pocket and handed them out to Tony. Resisting the urge to climb out to see for herself she said, 'What is it, Tony?'

'The flying boat is back again, I said it would be.'

'What flare are you going to use?'

'The parachute will last longest. They're still heading this way, so the pilot should see it.'

Tony snapped the safety and held the flare at arm's length above his head. With a whoosh the projectile soared into the sky, creating a bright speck that, trailing a streamer of smoke, drifted slowly away on the breeze. Choking from the smoke Tony clamped the binoculars to his eyes. Detecting a slight change in the distant aircraft's attitude he reported, 'They've seen it.'

The others were crowding the entrances now eager for a glimpse of their rescuer and calling for another flare.

Tony resisted the demand. 'When they get closer, I'll use smoke.' These are all we have left and we aren't home and dry yet.' He waited until the distinctive orange stripe on the fuselage of the aircraft was clearly visible, before he succumbed to the pressure and fired the smoke flare.

The aircraft circled the raft three times then started to signal with a flashing light.

Adam Stone was demanding loudly why they were not landing already. Tony keeping his eyes on the flashing light translated the Morse in his head. Eventually he said, 'Shut up Adam and I'll tell you.' He waited until the crew had all quietened, then went on. They say they can't land in the swell but a rescue cutter from Bermuda is on its way and will be here in about five hours. They're dropping a powerful GPS marker buoy and some provisions to cheer us up. Help is on the way.'

Tony waved an acknowledgement at the plane which made one last circuit dropping a large object about two hundred yards away then turned away to the east. By the time they had paddled the cumbersome raft to the bobbing marker, the aircraft was lost from sight. They retrieved the package and tied the raft to the buoy with its annoying strobe light. Taking comfort from the bleeps of the radio signal calling to their rescuers, they set about having a celebratory lunch.

Adam was first to spot the dark and distant speck; but the excitement was not shared by all. Jack Brownlow had withdrawn into his shell again and some of the others had gone quiet. It was up to Ken Watts to voice what, to many of them, was on their minds.

'I, for one, didn't expect to come out of this so well,' he said. 'We have all revealed some aspects of ourselves that we would rather have kept private. Can I suggest that we all agree that what was said on the raft, stays on the raft.'

'Like in the confessional, eh Vicar?' Diana piped up.

'We don't have that luxury in the protestant faith, my dear,' Goodfellow replied, 'but I take your point.'

So it was settled, not with a swearing of oaths, just a general agreement between equally invested partners.

Ken settled back alongside Diana and spoke hesitantly, in a low voice, 'Diana, I know that we didn't get off to a good start . . . but I was . . . wondering if . . . when we are rescued . . . would you consider letting me take you out to dinner?

Diana, astonished and flattered at the same time at his suggestion, replied, 'Yes, that is of course . . .'

'I completely understand if you say no, in view of the fact that I . . . have been so rude to you,' Ken went on humbly.

'Yes, I said yes, but are you sure you can trust me not to leave any explosive devices under the table?

'You will have to search me to make sure, won't you?' she said provocatively.

'That's no problem. I'll get Maxine on the job'

'Who is Maxine?' Her face darkened, 'because if she's your wife or anything, forget it!'

'Ha ha, Maxine is my German Shepherd, a retired police dog.'

'Oh you . . .'

The Bermudan coastguard cutter, oh so slowly, grew larger as it approached. They all returned to their own thoughts in the hour or so it took to come alongside.

The smiles of the crew, as they helped them on board could never match those of the survivors. The elation was tempered with concern as they enquired about their missing loved ones. While they were given warm drinks and the worst of their sores and injuries cleaned and treated before donning the luxury of dry clothes they were assured that the majority of the passengers and crew of the Eco Star were accounted for and safe in Miami. The cutter's commanding officer took great pains to find out from the rescue coordination centre about their individual relatives.

Once ashore, they would have to face the Bermudan customs officials but until then, they could relax and enjoy the ride.

Sitting in the wardroom in ones and twos they chatted quietly or relaxed in the firm but comfortable chairs and tried to get some sleep, at last without the threat of impending disaster to haunt their dreams.

The welcome by the Bermudan authorities was unequivocal but they all had to take turns being interviewed about their ordeal. It fell to Jenni (with an "i") to report the loss of Clarissa Sparrow who, as they all agreed to say, had fallen into the sea one night; an accident that was corroborated by each in turn.

The disappearance of Jack Brownlow, between disembarking from the cutter and their arrival at the customs office, was both perplexing and satisfying. The unspoken sentiment of them all was "Wherever you are, Jack, be good and be happy."

The End

Raft of Life

Lightning Source UK Ltd.
Milton Keynes UK
UKHW020748210722
406179UK00010B/1144

9 780957 452350